Belonging to God

Books by William C. Placher

A History of Christian Theology: An Introduction

Readings in the History of Christian Theology, Volume 1:
From Its Beginnings to the Eve of the Reformation

Readings in the History of Christian Theology, Volume 2:
From the Reformation to the Present

Unapologetic Theology: A Christian Voice
in a Pluralistic Conversation

Books by David Willis-Watkins

Daring Prayer

The Context of Contemporary Theology:
Essays in Honor of Paul Lehmann
(Edited with Alexander J. McKelway)

Belonging to God

A Commentary on
A Brief Statement of Faith

William C. Placher and David Willis-Watkins

Westminster/John Knox Press
Louisville, Kentucky

Scripture quotations from the New Revised Standard Version of the Bible are copyright © 1989 by the Division of Christian Education of the National Council of the Churches of Christ in the U.S.A., and are used by permission.

Book design by Denominational Resources/Publications Service

First edition

Published by Westminster/John Knox Press
Louisville, Kentucky

This book is printed on acid-free paper that meets the American National Standards Institute Z39.48 standard. ∞

PRINTED IN THE UNITED STATES OF AMERICA

9 8 7 6 5 4 3 2 1

Library of Congress Cataloging-in-Publication Data

Placher, William C. (William Carl), 1948–
    Belonging to God : a commentary on A brief statement of faith /
William C. Placher & David Willis-Watkins. — 1st ed.
        p.   cm.
    Includes bibliographical references and indexes.
    ISBN 0-664-25296-6 (alk. paper)

    1. Presbyterian Church (U.S.A.). Brief statement of faith.
2. Presbyterian Church (U.S.A.)—Creeds. 3. Presbyterian Church—
United States—Creeds. 4. Reformed Church—United States—Creeds.
I. Willis-Watkins, David. II. Presbyterian Church (U.S.A.). Brief statement
of faith. 1992. III. Title.
BX8969.5.P53 1992
238'.5137—dc20   91-48344

Contents

Preface

"You go to that church down the street. What do you believe? What does your church teach?"

Presbyterians often have a hard time answering questions like that. We quite rightly try to avoid slogans or overly simple formulas to describe our faith, but as a result we sometimes find ourselves almost unable to give any account of it at all. A "statement of faith" or a "confession" provides one starting point for setting out, and for thinking about, what we believe. In 1991 the Presbyterian Church (U.S.A.) adopted a new "Brief Statement of Faith" to join the nine other documents in our *Book of Confessions,* which is the first part of our church's constitution.

Presbyterians stand in a tradition—and a worldwide community—of "Reformed" Christianity, which began with John Calvin and other Reformers in the sixteenth century. Reformed Christians have regularly written new statements of what we believe—that is one of the ways in which our tradition differs from, say, the Lutherans' or the Roman Catholics'. One recent collection includes several dozen confessions adopted by Reformed churches around the world in just the last forty years.[1] This Brief Statement of Faith is one of the newest and shortest of such confessional documents. Taking up only about two pages of print, it is a contemporary effort by Presbyterians in the United States to say, briefly and clearly, to ourselves, our neighbors, and the rest of the world: This is who we are, this is what we believe.

One of the characteristics of who we are is that we are people who *think* about our faith. Back in the earliest days of the

Reformed churches, the literacy rate usually increased dramatically when Reformed Christians began to exercise influence in a particular country. They set up schools and taught people, all the people, to read so that they could study the Bible and other religious texts for themselves. The Brief Statement of Faith is, among other things, an invitation to thinking for ourselves—to discussion and even debate about the densely packed lines of this relatively brief text. This commentary is designed to help in that process.

In understanding any piece of writing, it usually helps to know something about the situation that produced it. So, how did this Brief Statement of Faith come into existence?

In 1983 the two largest groups of Presbyterians in the United States reunited to form a new church body, the Presbyterian Church (U.S.A.). The United Presbyterian Church in the U.S.A. (mostly in the North) and the Presbyterian Church in the U.S. (mostly in the South) had been divided since the Civil War, and they had come to have, among their other differences, different confessional standards. In the UPCUSA, pastors and elders had promised at their ordinations to be "guided" by a book of nine confessions, beginning with the Apostles' and Nicene creeds, and running through a number of Reformation documents to the more recent Barmen Declaration and Confession of 1967. The PCUS had kept the Westminster Confession and Shorter Catechism, written in seventeenth-century England, as its confessional basis, together with an interpretive summary of them written in 1962, "A Brief Statement of Belief."

The unity of a church, most people seemed to agree, should not consist simply in having a common bureaucratic structure or a single set of rules for settling disputes. What above all unites a *church* ought to be its confession of a common faith. The Plan for Reunion therefore directed the appointment of a committee to prepare "a brief statement of Reformed faith for possible inclusion in the *Book of Confessions.*" Accordingly, in May of 1984 J. Randolph Taylor, Moderator of the 1983 General Assembly, appointed a committee of twenty-one persons to draft such a statement. Your authors served as two members of that committee.

To make a very long story short, five years and many meetings later our committee unanimously recommended a new "Brief Statement of Faith" to the 1989 General Assembly. That Assembly debated our work, suggested a few minor changes, and, as required by the *Book of Order*, appointed a "Committee of Fifteen" (which actually had sixteen members) to review the document during the following year. They made small but significant revisions, and their revised version was approved by the 1990 General Assembly—over 90 percent of the votes in favor. The next stage required for ratification was approval by two thirds of the presbyteries. In fact, during early 1991, 166 presbyteries voted in favor, two against. The 1991 General Assembly in Baltimore voted final approval (412 in favor, 40 opposed, 16 abstentions), and this document now becomes part of the confessional heritage of our denomination.

Somewhere along the way, the title changed. The original assignment was to produce "A Brief Statement of *Reformed* Faith." (Emphasis added. Frequently in this study words quoted from the Brief Statement have been italicized for emphasis.) But the Reformers themselves would probably have been bothered by defining the task in just that way. They would have thought that the goal of any statement of faith ought to be to lay out "biblical" faith or the "catholic" (that is, universal) faith of Christians. The committees working on this text came to share that conviction. To be sure, this question of distinctiveness raises complicated issues. As the Preface to the Brief Statement puts it, "We are convinced that to the Reformed Churches a distinctive vision of the catholic faith has been entrusted for the good of the whole Church."

On the one hand, then, we Presbyterians have a "*distinctive vision.*" Our particular tradition within Christianity has had some distinctive emphases, and we think they are matters of importance. Our *Book of Order* gives one list of them (G-2.0300–2.0500). After identifying belief in "[1] the mystery of the triune God and [2] of the incarnation of the eternal Word of God in Jesus Christ" as beliefs we share with *Christians* generally, it mentions the principles of [3] grace alone, [4] faith alone, and [5] scripture alone as themes important to all *Protestants.* Then it singles out

[6] The election of the people of God for service as well as for
salvation; [7] Covenant life marked by a disciplined concern for
order in the church according to the Word of God; [8] A faithful stewardship that shuns ostentation and seeks proper use of
the gifts of God's creation; and [9] The recognition of the
human tendency to idolatry and tyranny, which calls the people
of God to work for the transformation of society by seeking justice and living in obedience to the Word of God

as distinctive themes of the *Reformed* tradition within Protes-
tantism.

Presbyterian historians and theologians might not all agree
on exactly that list, but these are certainly ideas that appear
prominently in the Reformed tradition from the time of Calvin
and Zwingli until today: Our "salvation," we believe, ought to
make a difference in the way we live our lives, and that difference ought to include living as part of orderly church communities, trying not to be wasteful of the good things in God's
creation, rejecting human individuals or institutions that set
themselves up as "idols" to be worshiped as if they were God,
and working for justice in our societies. Those are all themes
that appear in the Brief Statement.

On the other hand, these are not ideas unique to Reformed
Christians. Roman Catholics or Lutherans, for instance, would
remind us that they believe these things too! Diversity need
not imply disagreement. We often see that in a smaller way in
our own congregations. There are some people who always insist on the importance of balancing the church budget, and
others who keep reminding us of the need to support foreign
missions, and still others who regularly call attention to people
close at hand who need our help. Everyone is right, and our
church would be weaker if any of those voices were silenced.
Each group needs to make its emphasis as a contribution to the
whole, but it also needs to listen to the other points. Similarly,
we Presbyterians as a whole do have a distinctive perspective on
Christian faith—the passage just quoted from the *Book of Order*
suggests some of its elements—but we should not cling to our
distinctiveness, but rather offer it as a contribution to ongoing
discussions among all Christians. To quote the Preface of the
Brief Statement again:

We are thankful that in our time the many Churches are learning to accept, and even to affirm, diversity without divisiveness,
since the whole counsel of God is more than the wisdom of any
individual or any one tradition. The Spirit of Truth gives new
light to the Churches when they are willing to become pupils
together of the Word of God. This statement therefore intends
to confess the catholic faith.

We have a distinctive vision, but we believe it to be a vision of
the one *catholic faith*. We want to learn from other Christians;
but we want the richest possible conversation, and that means
we want to make sure that we too have something special and
worthwhile to contribute to it. That means holding on to special themes within our Reformed tradition, but it also means
that if this Statement is intended to join a general conversation
among all Christians, then a title that claims only to be describing what our particular tradition believes—"*Reformed* faith"—
seems inadequate; so the final text was headed simply "A Brief
Statement of Faith."

The goals of the statement, then, were inclusive, and so was
the process that produced it. Both committees included women
and men, ranging in age from their thirties to their seventies,
and with a variety of theological points of view. Members included African Americans, Hispanic Americans, European
Americans, native Americans, and Korean Americans. But the
committees also reached beyond their own membership for advice. As our committee was drafting the document, we held
hearings throughout the country and at several General
Assemblies, and we sent out a draft version to which we received over seventeen thousand responses.

Many of those responses did not simply come from individuals but grew out of the trial use of the statement in worship,
leadership training, and discussions in local congregations.
More was at stake, therefore, than just an effort at being demo-
cratic—for this was a case where the worshiping and teaching
experience of congregations had an influence on the wording
with which the faith is reconfessed, as the tested results, and
corrections, of their experience bore fruit in some significant
changes in the final text. Some of the responses were tallied by
computer, but at least one member of the committee read each

written comment, ranging from a few words to several pages of single-spaced typing. One should not write confessions by opinion poll, but a confession ought to confess the faith of the church, and that means, among other things, that those who write confessions need to hear the concerns, the joys, and the pains of the church's people.

The reunion had provided the *occasion* for a new statement of faith, but it was not obvious that it offered an adequate *reason*. Early on, our committee seriously debated whether we ought to undertake the task. For one thing, twenty-one people meeting in the basement of a motel near the Chicago airport felt inevitably intimidated at the thought of producing a document to take a place beside the classic products of the saints and martyrs and theological geniuses of the past. For another, the church faced no obvious specific crisis that would require a new spelling out of our faith.

At least for the two of us, the authors of this commentary, it was reflection on the history of earlier confessions and on what we heard as we listened to people around the church that persuaded us of the value of undertaking this assignment. Specific crises have provided the occasion for some confessional statements—the Arian controversy for the Nicene Creed in the fourth century, or the Nazi challenge for the Barmen Declaration in the 1930s. But other confessional documents have become important only gradually as they functioned in liturgy or teaching in the life of the church—the Apostles' Creed, for instance, or the Second Helvetic Confession. In our case, the "crisis," if that is the right word, seemed to concern precisely the ongoing life of the church. Is it possible to reconfess the most central teaching of the church in the face of the wide diversity, pluralism, and regionalism of contemporary society and the church today? The Confession of 1967, for example, acknowledged the centrality of the doctrines of the Trinity and the Person of Christ, but left them to function as presuppositions. A generation later, we can no longer take those doctrines, or the words we use to confess them, for granted. Can we confess them today in ways congruent with the needs of our pluralistic society and church? What, if anything, does a reconfession of the faith have to say to issues on which the church cannot remain confessionally silent, such as the ecological crisis, the need to speak with more sensitivity to gender-inclusiveness, the threat that nuclear arms pose for the future of the planet? These crises were not as precipitate or as dramatically inescapable as those which occasioned some of the earlier documents in the *Book of Confessions*. But it does not take a single dramatic moment of crisis to call forth a confession. What matters is that a text somehow serve a useful function in the life of a faithful community.

If one thinks about the life of the church today, then there does seem a good case to be made for a new statement of faith. Pastors from all over the country often talked to us about the need in the congregations for a basic introduction to Presbyterian beliefs. In many congregations, most of the members did not grow up Presbyterian. Our culture, and even our church education, cannot be counted on to provide even minimal familiarity with the Bible or Christian doctrines. Presbyterians ordained as elders promise to be "guided" by the *Book of Confessions,* but it is a large and intimidating document. They need an entry point, some place to start in thinking about what we believe.

Further, at a time when many of us are growing more sensitive to the way the language we use shapes our attitudes toward women and men, the language of the earlier documents in the *Book of Confessions* seems to be unremittingly male. Even the Confession of 1967, fairly recent and in its day passionately sensitive to matters of oppression and injustice, talks about "men" rather than "people," and "brothers" but not "sisters," to say nothing of its language about God. As a result, many congregations have been writing their own statements of faith, some deeply moving, some arguably rather odd. But even the good ones risk encouraging the perception that we no longer have a church that can confess a common faith.

So, we needed a text that would enter the life of the church, and that meant something usable in liturgy and in teaching. Both kinds of use seemed important. Church members wanting to learn about what we believe needed something teachable, but it would be most exciting to discuss in a class not some piece of paper that appeared there for the first time, but a document people had already encountered in the life of the community, ideally in worship. If one has gotten in the habit of saying a set of words, it is natural to want to reflect more about what they mean and why we say them. Use in the context of worship helps make a statement part of the language we use together. In a church where we are often conscious of a range of issues that divide us, we need something that will help us rediscover that we *can* confess together what we believe. If such a statement can enter and help shape the life of the church over the years, it may make a far more important contribution than would a dramatic response to some particular issue. In the context of the work of our committee, that meant we needed something reasonably short, something that sounded well when read aloud, something accessible to a wide range of church members, but also something complex enough to repay careful study.

The statement that resulted has five sections—an introduction, a conclusion, and three middle segments. The introduction affirms our faith in the triune God. It is with God that our faith begins, but not God simply as a philosophical principle or an abstract creator who has lost interest in creation. Rather, this is a gracious, loving God, who watches over and sustains creation, who reconciles and redeems us, who is at work among us. Christians down the centuries have encountered God as—to use the traditional terms—"Father," "Son," and "Holy Spirit." Moreover, they have believed that in these encounters they came to know God as God really is. There is not some utterly unitary God behind three manifestations of God: God really is triune, one God in three Persons. That Trinitarian faith provides the starting point and the organizational structure to this Brief Statement as it does to many earlier confessions.

The opening words of the introduction signal one of the important themes of the whole statement: "In life and in death . . ." A faith offering hope that stops short at death isn't good enough. It would not only fail to respond to our fears about what lies beyond death, it would distort what needs to be confessed about life here and now. Every day we face forces of death, powers that could kill us by deliberate plan or random whim. If our faith in the triune God does not somehow transcend even death, then we would have to find ways of placating those forces, and the triune God could not be the One "whom *alone* we worship and serve" (line 6). This Statement, therefore, begins by saying that we be-

long to God "in life *and* in death" (line 1), and concludes by rejoicing "that nothing in life or in death can separate us from the
love of God in Christ Jesus our Lord" (lines 78–79).

After the introductory affirmation of our trust in the triune
God in life and in death, each of the three middle sections of the
statement (lines 7–26, 27–51, 52–76) speaks of one Person of
the Trinity. Those sections also share a common structure. Each
begins with the good news of God's love for us: "Jesus proclaimed the reign of God" (line 9). "In sovereign love God created the world good" (line 29). "The Holy Spirit, everywhere the
giver and renewer of life[,] . . . justifies us by grace through faith"
(lines 52–54). Then each section turns to a confession of human
failures and sins: "Jesus was crucified" (line 20). "But we rebel
against God; we hide from our Creator" (line 33). "In a broken
and fearful world" there are "idolatries in Church and culture"
and peoples whose voices have been "long silenced" (lines 65,
69–70). Finally, each of these sections affirms that, in spite of our
faithlessness, God remains faithful, and therefore we can live in
hope: "God raised this Jesus from the dead" (line 23). "God is
faithful still" (line 51). We are "empowered by the Spirit, . . .
even as we watch for God's new heaven and new earth" (lines 72,
75). That note of hope leads back to the trust that sustains us in
life and in death which appears in the conclusion, together with a
final proclamation of the glory of God.

A commentary is always *one* interpretation, and carries with it
the invitation to its readers to reinterpret a text for themselves.
Since both of us served on the committee that drafted this
Statement, it is particularly important to make clear that this is
not an "official" commentary; we were not in any way commissioned by either committee or any General Assembly to write it.
We have not submitted it to the other members of the committees or to any official church body for approval. We hope that
what we have written will help people begin to think about this
Statement and about what our church believes, but others, even
others on the committees that produced this Statement, would
come up with different interpretations and emphases.

In our own writing in this commentary we have tried to be
sensitive to issues about gender and language. We have quoted
the Bible in the New Revised Standard Version, which corrects

male language introduced by earlier translations but not present in the original Hebrew or Greek. In quoting earlier confessions, Calvin, or other theologians, however, we have simply quoted the original text or the standard translation, only occasionally noting the male bias of the language. These are documents of their times. They have much to teach us still, but there is no point in pretending that they were written in awareness of all the issues that concern us in our time.

The two of us have both worked through the entire text of this commentary, but David Willis-Watkins initially wrote chapters 1–3 and 10–13, while William Placher initially wrote chapters 4–9 and 14.

We hope that this commentary will help our fellow Presbyterians—new members, new elders, or just interested church people—in local churches study the statement together. It may be useful for seminarians preparing for ministry or for pastors thinking about that important Reformed role, the teaching ministry. Beyond that, this commentary, like the Statement on which it comments, represents an effort to interpret Christian faith for today in a straightforward and understandable way. While the particular content of the Brief Statement shaped our work, we found ourselves having almost to write a short course in theology. We hope that non-Presbyterians too might find the results a useful introduction to thoughtful Christian belief.

William C. Placher
David Willis-Watkins

Acknowledgments

Quotations from Calvin's *Institutes* come from the Library of Christian Classics edition, translated by Ford Lewis Battles and edited by John T. McNeill (Philadelphia: Westminster Press, 1960). We are grateful to the publisher for permission to quote from this work. We are also grateful to the Office of the General Assembly for permission to quote from the *Book of Confessions*; we have indicated those passages with the numerical references to the sections in parentheses.

William Placher would also like to express his thanks to Edgar Perkins, Dale Robb, Steven Shoemaker, Maynard Strothmann, and Laurence Sunkel of the Reformed Roundtable, who read his chapters in an earlier draft and made most thoughtful and helpful comments; to Jeff Marlett, who organized Placher's files so that he could find things; and to the Eric Dean Fund of Wabash College for financial support for this work.

David Willis-Watkins would also like to thank Mary Hockenberry, member of the 201st General Assembly Standing Committee on the Brief Statement of Faith and former Moderator of Newton Presbytery; Stephen and Cynthia Strickler, and Sally Willis-Watkins and various members of the Wharton, New Jersey, United Presbyterian Church for their helpful discussions and suggestions; and Princeton Theological Seminary for financial support for this work.

We mean what we say in the Preface: This is not an "official" document but our own interpretation, for which we alone are responsible. At the same time, we are clear that we could not have written it without having gone through the remarkable process that produced this Statement. We are therefore grateful to the thousands of people around the church who made comments and raised hard questions over the years of the development of this Statement; to the committees of several successive General Assemblies who debated the Statement so thoughtfully; to the Committee of Fifteen, who worked hard to improve it in the face of all the protective instincts of its original "parents"; and above all to the other members of the Special Committee to Prepare a Brief Statement of Reformed Faith. This Statement really is that unlikely creature—a document written by a committee, often line by line and word by word. Every member made an important contribution, and out of all our diversity we ended up with a unanimous recommendation. Over five years, the committee became a locus for tough debate, a running seminar on Reformed theology, and a kind of family.

Suggestions for Use in Liturgy and Teaching

As a wide range of people expressed their reactions to various drafts of the Brief Statement of Faith, the most common comment took this form: "It's too long, but here's something else you have to include." The Statement in its entirety takes no longer to say than a long hymn takes to sing, but many congregations find it too long to recite together at one time. Educational and liturgical use, however, do seem tied together. People will be more interested in studying a document they have already encountered in worship. We would neither expect nor hope that this statement would replace the Apostles' Creed in churches where that has served as the usual affirmation of faith, but it could be helpful to use it in worship from time to time, perhaps during periods when there are classes for new members, for instance, or during certain seasons of the year. Some suggestions for such use:

1. The introduction, any one of the three middle sections, and the conclusion form a good statement of more manageable length (lines 1–6, 7–26, 77–80; or 1–6, 27–51, 77–80; or 1–6, 52–76, 77–80). Such use on three consecutive Sundays could then introduce the whole Statement.

2. It sometimes works better to have a leader and the congregation read alternate lines.

3. One can use parts of the Statement at various points in the service: for instance, lines 1–6 as a call to worship or invocation; lines 27–51 as a confession of sin and assurance of pardon;

lines 52–64 as a prayer for illumination; lines 7–26 as an affirmation of faith; lines 65–76 as a prayer of dedication; and lines 77–80 as a benediction. Others will want to use only portions of those sections.

We have tried to design this commentary to help in the educational uses of the Statement. There are fourteen chapters. A class discussing the Statement could spend one week on each chapter, one week on each two chapters, or cover the whole in three weeks (chapters 1–5, 6–9, 10–14). Our experience is that the Statement itself generates discussion. One need only read a few lines aloud together and ask why this word, why this order, what seems left out—and one has a lively conversation. The appended cross-references for each line to scripture and the *Book of Confessions* invite people to use this Statement as a starting point for study of the Bible and earlier confessions, and it is our hope that this commentary will open further discussion, both to the theological tradition and to a range of contemporary issues.

A Brief Statement of Faith— Presbyterian Church (U.S.A.)

Preface[1]

In 1983 the two largest Presbyterian churches in the United States reunited. *The Plan for Reunion* called for the preparation of a brief statement of the Reformed faith for possible inclusion in the *Book of Confessions*. This statement is therefore not intended to stand alone, apart from the other confessions of our Church. It does not pretend to be a complete list of all our beliefs, nor does it explain any of them in detail. It is designed to be confessed by the whole congregation in the setting of public worship, and it may also serve pastors and teachers as an aid to Christian instruction. It celebrates our rediscovery that for all our undoubted diversity, we are bound together by a common faith and a common task.

The faith we confess unites us with the one, universal Church. The most important beliefs of Presbyterians are those we share with other Christians, and especially with other evangelical Christians who look to the Protestant Reformation as a renewal of the gospel of Jesus Christ. Diversity remains. But we are thankful that in our time the many Churches are learning to accept, and even to affirm, diversity without divisiveness, since the whole counsel of God is more than the wisdom of any individual or any one tradition. The Spirit of Truth gives new light to the Churches when they are willing to become pupils together of the Word of God. This statement therefore intends to confess the catholic faith.

[1]The preface and the appendix do not have confessional authority.

We are convinced that to the Reformed churches a distinctive vision of the catholic faith has been entrusted for the good of the whole Church. Accordingly, A Brief Statement of Faith includes the major themes of the Reformed tradition (such as those mentioned in the *Book of Order,* "Form of Government," Chapter 2),[2] without claiming them as our private possession, just as we ourselves hope to learn and to share the wisdom and insight given to traditions other than our own. And as a confession that seeks to be both catholic and Reformed, the statement (following the apostle's blessing in 2 Cor. 13:14) is a trinitarian confession in which the grace of Jesus Christ has first place as the foundation of our knowledge of God's sovereign love and our life together in the Holy Spirit.

No confession of faith looks merely to the past; every confession seeks to cast the light of a priceless heritage on the needs of the present moment, and so to shape the future. Reformed confessions, in particular, when necessary even re-form the tradition itself in the light of the Word of God. From the first, the Reformed Churches have insisted that the renewal of the Church must become visible in the transformation of human lives and societies. Hence A Brief Statement of Faith lifts up concerns that call most urgently for the Church's attention in our time. The Church is not a refuge from the world; an elect people is chosen for the blessing of the nations. A sound confession, therefore, proves itself as it nurtures commitment to the Church's mission, and as the confessing Church itself becomes the body by which Christ continues the blessing of his earthly ministry.

---

[2]The appendix provides cross-references which will enable the reader to place the affirmations of A Brief Statement of Faith in context of the Reformed tradition.

A Brief Statement of Faith—
Presbyterian Church (U.S.A.)

1   In life and in death we belong to God.
2   Through the grace of our Lord Jesus Christ,
3   the love of God,
4   and the communion of the Holy Spirit,
5   we trust in the one triune God, the Holy One of Israel,
6   whom alone we worship and serve.

7   We trust in Jesus Christ,
8   fully human, fully God.
9   Jesus proclaimed the reign of God:
10   preaching good news to the poor
11   and release to the captives,
12   teaching by word and deed
13   and blessing the children,
14   healing the sick
15   and binding up the brokenhearted,
16   eating with outcasts,
17   forgiving sinners,
18   and calling all to repent and believe the gospel.
19   Unjustly condemned for blasphemy and sedition,
20   Jesus was crucified,
21   suffering the depths of human pain
22   and giving his life for the sins of the world.
23   God raised this Jesus from the dead,
24   vindicating his sinless life,
25   breaking the power of sin and evil,
26   delivering us from death to life eternal.

27 We trust in God,
28   whom Jesus called Abba, Father.
29   In sovereign love God created the world good
30   and makes everyone equally in God's image,
31   male and female, of every race and people,
32   to live as one community.
33   But we rebel against God; we hide from our Creator.
34   Ignoring God's commandments,

35   we violate the image of God in others and ourselves,
36   accept lies as truth,
37   exploit neighbor and nature,
38   and threaten death to the planet entrusted to our care.
39   We deserve God's condemnation.
40   Yet God acts with justice and mercy to redeem creation.
41   In everlasting love,
42   the God of Abraham and Sarah chose a covenant people
43   to bless all families of the earth.
44   Hearing their cry,
45   God delivered the children of Israel
46   from the house of bondage.
47   Loving us still,
48   God makes us heirs with Christ of the covenant.
49   Like a mother who will not forsake her nursing child,
50   like a father who runs to welcome the prodigal home,
51   God is faithful still.

52   We trust in God the Holy Spirit,
53   everywhere the giver and renewer of life.
54   The Spirit justifies us by grace through faith,
55   sets us free to accept ourselves and to love God and neighbor,
56   and binds us together with all believers
57   in the one body of Christ, the Church.
58   The same Spirit
59   who inspired the prophets and apostles
60   rules our faith and life in Christ through Scripture,
61   engages us through the Word proclaimed,
62   claims us in the waters of baptism,
63   feeds us with the bread of life and the cup of salvation,
64   and calls women and men to all ministries of the Church.
65   In a broken and fearful world
66   the Spirit gives us courage
67   to pray without ceasing,
68   to witness among all peoples to Christ as Lord and Savior,
69   to unmask idolatries in Church and culture,
70   to hear the voices of peoples long silenced,
71   and to work with others for justice, freedom, and peace.
72   In gratitude to God, empowered by the Spirit,

73   we strive to serve Christ in our daily tasks
74   and to live holy and joyful lives,
75   even as we watch for God's new heaven and new earth,
76   praying, "Come, Lord Jesus!"

77 With believers in every time and place,
78   we rejoice that nothing in life or in death
79   can separate us from the love of God in Christ Jesus our Lord.

80   Glory be to the Father, and to the Son, and to the Holy Spirit.
        Amen.*

        *Instead of saying this line, congregations may wish to sing a version of the Gloria.

Cross-References

The writers of A Brief Statement of Faith have endeavored to establish this confession on the broad base of Scripture as a whole and the consensus of Reformed theology, not upon isolated or particular texts either in Scripture or theology.

These cross-references identify sources that have significantly shaped the specific part of the faith being confessed at the lines indicated. They show the congruence of A Brief Statement of Faith with the teachings of the Scriptures and of earlier confessional documents. They point to only a selected few of the passages and contexts that congregations could study in comparing the ways the faith has been re-confessed in diverse historical situations.

The verse references and abbreviations for books of the Bible are based on the *Revised Standard Version*. Biblical passages are listed in the order of their occurrence in the English Bible, except that parallel passages from the Synoptic Gospels (Matthew, Mark, and Luke) have been grouped together. Portions of the verses cited in italics are quoted or closely paraphrased in A Brief Statement of Faith.

Documents in the *Book of Confessions* are abbreviated as follows: NC, Nicene Creed; AC, Apostles' Creed; SC, Scots Confession; HC, Heidelberg Catechism; SHC, Second Helvetic Confession; WCF, Westminster Confession of Faith [numbered according to the edition used by the former United

Presbyterian Church (U.S.A.)]; WSC, Westminster Shorter
Catechism; WLC, Westminster Larger Catechism; BD,
Theological Declaration of Barmen; C67, Confession of 1967.

Citations are listed in the order of their occurrence in the
Book of Confessions.

Lines 1–6

1	Scripture	Deut 7:6–11; Ps 100; 139:1–12; Is 43:1–9; Jer 31; Rom 8:31–39; 14:7–9; 2 Cor 5:1–5.
	Confessions	SC, 1; HC, q 1; WLC, q 1; BD, II, 1, 2.
2–6	Scripture	Ex 20:3–6; Deut 6:4–9; 11:16; 2 Kings 19:14–22; Ps 56:3–4; 62:1–8; 71:22–24; 103; Is 10:20; 12:5–6; 17:7–8; 43:14–15; 54:5; Jer 17:5–8; 25:5–6; Dan 3:28; Mt 28:16–20; Jn 3:16; 14:8–17; Acts 2:41–42; 27:21–26; 1 Cor 8:1–6; *2 Cor 13:14;* Eph 2:8–10; 1 Pet 1:2–9.
	Confessions	NC; SC, I, IV; HC, q 25; SHC, III, V; WCF, II, VII, 5; WSC, q 6; WLC, qq 6–11; C67, "The Confession," IA–C.

Lines 7–26

7–8	Scripture	Ps 86:1–2; Is 12:2; Mt 1:18–25; 11:27; Mk 8:27–30; 14:61–62; Lk 2:1–52; Jn 1:1–18; 5:1–18; 7:25–31; 10:30–39; Gal 4:1–7; Phil 2:5–11; Col 1:15–20; 2:8–10; Heb 1; 2:14–18; 4:14–15; 5:7–10; 13:8; 1 Jn 1:1–2.
	Confessions	NC, 2nd art.; SC, VI; HC, qq 31, 35, 47; SHC, XI; WCF, VIII, 2; WSC, q 21; WLC, qq 36–42; C67, IA1.
9–18	Scripture	Ps 34:6–18; 146:5–9; 147:1–6; Is 42:1–7; *61:1*–3; Ezek 34:15–16; Zeph 3:19; Mt 4:23–25; 9:10–13; 13:1–58; 15:21–28; 18:21–35; 23:1–4; Mk

1:14–15; 5:1–20; 6:30–44; 9:33–37; 10:13–16; Lk *4:16–22 (18);* 5:17–32; 6:17–36; 7:1–27, 33–50; 8:1–3; 10:38–42; 15:1–32; Jn 4:1–42; 8:1–11; 10:1–8; 11:1–44; 16:33; Acts 10:34–43.

Confessions	SC, XIV, XVI; HC, qq 1, 31, 74, 107; SHC, XIII–XV; WCF, VIII, XII, XXV; WSC, qq 21–30, 36; WLC, qq 43–50, 135; BD, I; C67, IA1, IIA4c, III.

19–22	Scripture	
	Lines 19–20	Mt 26:57–68; Mk 14:53–65; Lk 22:63–71; Mt 27:32–37; Mk 15:21–26; Lk 23:32–35; Jn 10:22–39; 19:1–22; 1 Cor 1:20–25.
	Lines 21–22	Ps 22; 88:1–9; Is 52:13–53:12; Mt 27:27–31, 39–50; Mk 15:16–20, 29–37; Lk 23:11, 39–46; Mk 8:31–35; 10:45; Lk 22:39–46; Jn 1:29–34; 3:16–18; 10:7–18; 19:28–37; Rom 5; 2 Cor 5:17–21; 1 Tim 2:5–6; Heb 2; 5:7–10; 9:11–22; 1 Pet 2:21–24; 3:18; 1 Jn 2:1–2; 4:9–10; Rev 5.
	Confessions	SC, VIII, IX; HC, qq 29–44; SHC, XI; WCF, VIII; WSC, qq 28–31; WLC, qq 44, 49.

23–26	Scripture	
	Lines 23–24	Ps 24:4–5; 26:1; 37:5–6; Is 50:4–9; Mt 27:3–4; 28:1–17; Mk 16:1–8; Lk 24:1–47; Jn 20–21; Acts 2:22–36 *(32);* 17:16–34; Rom 1:1–7; 1 Cor 15:3–57; 1 Tim 3:14–16.
	Lines 25–26	Ps 49:13–15; Is 25:6–8; Dan 12:2–3; Jn 3:16–18; 5:19–24; 11:17–27; Rom 4:24–25; 5:1–21; 6:1–23; 8:1–11; 1 Cor 15:20–28; Eph 2:1–7; Col 1:9–14; 2:8–15; 1 Thess 4:13–18; 2 Tim 1:10; Heb 13:20–21; Rev 21:3–4.

| | Confessions | SC, X; HC, qq 45–52; SHC, XI; WCF, VIII, 4–8; WLC, qq 52–56; BD, II, 2–4; C67, IA1. |

Lines 27–51

| 27–28 | Scripture | 2 Kings 18:5–6; Ps 28:6–7; 71:5–6; Prov 3:5–8; Mt 6:25–34; *Mk 14:32–36;* Lk 11:2–4; Rom 8:12–17; Gal 4:1–7. |
| | Confessions | NC, 1st art.; AC, 1st art.; HC, qq 26–28; WCF, XII; WLC, q 100. |

29–32	Scripture	
	Line 29	Gen 1:1–25; Ps 33:1–9; 104; Is 40:21–28; Jn 1:1–5; Col 1:15–20; 1 Tim 4:4.
	Lines 30–32	Gen 1:26–2:25; 5:1–32 (esp. 1–5, 32); 10:32–11:1; Lev 19:9–18; Ps 22:25–31; 67; 133; Is 56:3–8; 66:18–21; Mic 4:1–4; Lk 10:29–37; Acts 17:22–28; Eph 1:9–10; Rev 7:9–12; 22:1–2.
	Confessions	HC, q 6; SHC, VII; WCF, IV, 1–2; WSC, qq 9, 10; WLC, qq 12–17; C67, IIA4a.

33–38	Scripture	
	Line 33	Gen 3:1–24; 4:1–6; Ex 3:6; 4:1–17; Judg 11:29–40; 1 Sam 10:20–24; Ps 2:1–3; 14:1–4; Is 1:1–6; Jer 5:20–25; 23–24; Jon 1:1–4; Mt 5:14–16; Mk 4:21–23; Lk 8:16–18; Mt 19:16–22; 25:14–30 (esp. 18, 24–25); Lk 8:43–48; 10:38–42 (Martha); Rom 1:16–3:26; Heb 4:13; Rev 2–3; 6:12–17.
	Line 34	Gen 1:28; 2:15–16; Ex 20:1–17; 21:1–23:19; Lev 19:1–37; Deut 6:4–9; 10:19; Neh 7:73b–8:18; Ps 119:169–176; Amos 5:24; Mic 6:8; Mt 5:17–6:21; 7:12; 22:34–40; Jn 13:34;

		14:15; 15:12–17; Rom 13:8–10; 1 Cor 8; 1 Jn 2:3–11.
	Line 35	Gen 1:27; 4:8; 6:11–12; 16; 21:9–21; Judg 19; 2 Sam 11; 13:1–20; 18:5–15; Ps 14:1–4; Is 1:12–23; 59:1–8; Ezek 7:10–11; 45:9; Zeph 3:1–4; Mt 23:13–28; 25:31–46; Lk 16:19–31; Rom 1:28–32; Eph 4:17–22; Col 3:5–11; 2 Tim 3:1–9; Tit 1:15–16.
	Line 36	Gen 2:16–17; 3:1–4; Job 13:1–12; Ps 4:2; Is 5:20–21; 28:14–15; 59:3b, 12–15a; Jer 5:1–3; 14:13–14; Jn 8:42–45.
	Lines 37–38	Gen 2:15; Ps 8; Is 5:7–8; 24:4–6; 33:7–9; Jer 2:7–8; 9:4–6; Hos 4:1–3; Amos 2:6–8; Acts 16:16–24.
	Confessions	SC, II; HC, qq 3–11, 106, 107; SHC, VIII, IX; WCF, VI; WSC, q 77; WLC, qq 22–28, 105, 131, 132, 136, 145, 149; C67, IA2.
39	Scripture	Gen 6:5–7; Deut 28:15–68; 30:15–20; 2 Sam 12:1–12; Is 1:24–25; 5:9–10, 24–25; 28:16–22; 59:9–11, 15b–19; Jer 2:9; 9:7–11; 14:15–16; Amos 2:13–16; Jn 3:16–21; Rom 5:18–21; 8:1–4.
	Confessions	SC, III, XV; HC, qq 10–12; SHC, XII, XIII; WCF, VI, 6; WSC, qq 82–85; WLC, q 27; C67, IA2.
40	Scripture	2 Chron 7:11–14; Ps 34:22; 51; 78:36–39; 103:1–14; 130; 145:8–9; Is 2:2–4; 6:5–7; 11:1–9; 30:18; 51:4–6; Jer 31:20; Lam 3:22–33; Ezek 36:8–15; Hos 11:1–9; 14:4–8; Mt 1:18–21; Lk 1:67–79; 15:1–7; Jn 3:16–17; Rom 5:15–17; 8:18–25; Eph 2:4–7; 1 Pet 1:13–21.

	Confessions	SC, I, IV; HC, qq 26–28; SHC, VI, X; WCF, V; WSC, q 31; WLC, q 30.
41–51	Scripture	
	Lines 41–43	Gen 12:1–7; 15; 17:1–21; 18:1–15; 21:1–7; 28:10–17; Deut 7:6–7; Neh 9:6–8; Ps 65:1–4; Is 41:8–10; 44:1–8; 51:1–2; Jer 31:3, 31–34; Mt 9:9–13; 26:26–28; Rom 4:13–25; 11; 1 Cor 1:26–29; Gal 3:6–9; Eph 1:3–10; 1 Thess 1; Heb 11:8–12; Jas 2:5; 1 Pet 2:9–10.
	Lines 44–46	Ex 2:23–3:10; 6:2–8; 15:1–21; 18:5–12; 20:1–2; 22:21–24; Deut 7:8; Judg 6:7–16; 10:10–16; 2 Chron 32:9–23; Ezra 9:6–9; Neh 9:9–15; Ps 18:1–19; 34; 77; 105:23–45; 107; 136; Is 40:3–5, 9–11; 43:14–21; 51:9–16; Dan 3; 6; Mic 6:4; Mt 6:13; 15:21–28; Mk 5:1–20; 2 Cor 1:8–11; Rev 1:4–11; 15:2–4.
	Lines 47–48	Ps 33:20–22; 36:7–9; Is 54:4–10; 63:7–9; Mic 7:18–20; Mt 26:26–29; *Rom 8:15–17*, 38–39; 1 Cor 11:23–26; Gal 3:15–29; 4:6–7, 21–31; Eph 1:3–6; 2:11–22; Heb 13:20–21; 1 Pet 1:1–9; 1 Jn 3:1–2.
	Lines 49–51	Gen 33:1–11; Deut 7:9; 32:10–12; Neh 9:16–23; Ps 27:7–10; 36:5–12; 91; 117; Is 42:14–16; 46:3–4; 49:7; *49:14–15;* 66:13; Jer 31:15–20; Lam 3:22–23; Hos 11:3–4; Lk 13:34–35; 15:11–32 (esp. 20); *1 Cor 1:9;* 1 Thess 5:23–24; 2 Thess 2:16–17.
	Confessions	SC, IV, V; HC, qq 12–15, 18, 19, 34, 49, 51, 52, 54, 128; SHC, XIII, XVII–XIX; WCF, VI, 4, VII, VIII, 8, XVII, XVIII, XXXV, "Declaratory Statement" of 1903; WSC, q 36; WLC, qq 31–34, 74; BD, II, 2; C67, IB.

Lines 52–76

52–53	Scripture	Gen 1:1–2; Ps 23; 139:1–12; Ezek 37:1–14; Lk 1:26–35; Jn 3:1–15; Acts 2:1–21; 10; Rom 8:1–11; 2 Cor 3.
	Confessions	NC, 3rd art.; AC, 3rd art; SC, XII; HC, q 53; WCF, XX, XXXIV; WLC, qq 58, 89, 182.
54–57	Scripture Line 54	Gen 15:1–6; Hab 2:4; Rom 1:16–17; *3:21–28 (24–25);* 4:1–5; 5:1–2; Gal 3:1–14; Eph 2:8–9; Tit 3:3–7.
	Lines 55–57	Lev 19:18; Deut 6:4–5; Mk 12:28–34; Lk 10:25–37; Jn 3:1–15; Rom 8:26–27; 12; 13:8–10; 1 Cor 12:1–31 (esp. 13, 27); 13; 2 Cor 3:17–4:2; Gal 5; 6:1–10; Eph 2:11–22; 4:1–6; Phil 4:1–7; Col 1:24; 3:12–17; 1 Pet 4:8–11; 1 Jn 4:19–5:5.
	Confessions	SC, XVI–XX; HC, qq 1, 21, 54, 55, 86, 87; SHC, XV–XVII; WCF, XI, XX, XXV, XXVI, XXXIV, XXXV; WSC, qq 29–36; WLC, qq 63–66, 70–73; BD, II, 1–3; C67, IC1.
58–61	Scripture Lines 58–59	Num 11:24–30; Deut 18:15–22; 2 Chron 20:13–19; 24:20–22; Ezek 3:22–27; 8:1–4; 11:5–12; 13:3; Mic 3:5–8; Mk 12:35–37; Jn 20:19–23; Acts 1:1–9; 2:1–4; 9:17–19a; 1 Pet 1:10–11; 2 Pet 1:20–21.
	Lines 60–61	2 Kings 22:8–13; 23:1–3; Ps 119:1–16; Zech 7:11–12; Mt 5:17; Mk 13:9–11; Lk 24:13–27, 44; Jn 5:30–47; 16:13; Acts 2:14–36; 4:13–20; 8:4–8; 9:17–22; 10:34–44; 13:4–5; 17:1–4; Rom 15:17–21; Eph 2:19–3:6; 2 Tim 1:11–14;

		3:14–17; Heb 1:1–4; 3:7–11; 1 Pet 1:12; 2 Pet 1:16–19; 3:1–2; Rev 3:22.
	Confessions	SC, XIX, XX; HC, qq 19–21; SHC, I, II; WCF, I, XXXIV, 2; WSC, qq 2, 3; WLC, qq 2–6, 108; BD, I, II, 1; C67, IC2, IIB1.
62–64	Scripture Line 62	Mk 1:1–12; 6:30–52; Jn 1:19–34; 3:5; 7:37–39; Acts 2:38–42; 8:26–39; 9:10–19; 10:44–11:18; Rom 6:1–4; 1 Cor 12:12–13; Gal 3:27–28; Eph 1:13–14; Col 2:8–15; Tit 3:3–7; 1 Jn 5:6–8.
	Line 63	*Ps 116:12–14 (13);* Mt 26:17–29; Mk 14:22–25; Lk 22:14–20; 24:13–35; *Jn 6:22–59 (35, 48);* Acts 2:41–42; 1 Cor 10:16–17; 11:17–34; Heb 9:11–28.
	Line 64	Gen 1:26–27; Ex 15:1–21; Judg 4:4–10; 2 Kings 22:8–20; Joel 2:28–32; Lk 1:46–55; 2:25–38; 8:1–3; 10:38–42; Jn 4:7–42; 20; Acts 1:12–2:47; 13:1–4; 16:1–15; 18:24–28; Rom 16:1–16; 1 Cor 12:4–7; 2 Cor 4–5; Gal 3:27–29; Eph 4:7–16; Phil 4:1–3; 1 Pet 2:9–10.
	Confessions	SC, XVIII, XXI–XXIII; HC, qq 65–85; SHC, XVIII–XXVIII; WCF, XXVI–XXXI; WSC, qq 88–98; WLC, qq 157, 158, 164–177; BD, II, 1, 3–6; C67, IIA1–2, IIB.
65–71	Scripture Lines 65–66	Gen 15:1; Ps 23:1–4; 27:1–6; 46:1–3; Is 41:8–10; Hag 2:4–5; Acts 4:13–31; Phil 1:19–20; 2 Cor 1:18–22.
	Line 67	Gen 18:16–33; 2 Sam 7:18–29; Dan 6; Mt 6:5–15; Mk 14:32–42; Lk 18:1–8; Jn 17; Rom 12:12; Eph 6:18–20; Col

1:3–14; 4:2; *1 Thess* 5:16–18 *(17)*; Jas 5:13–18; Jude 20–21.

Line 68	Is 60:1–3; Mt 28:19–20; Lk 24:45–47; Acts 1:8; 9:27–29; 23:11; Rom 1:1–6; 1 Thess 2:1–8; 2 Tim 1:8–14; 4:1–2.
Line 69	Ex 20:2–6; 1 Kings 18:21–39; Ps 115:1–11; Is 31:1–3; 44:6–20; Jer 7:1–20; Zech 4:6; Mt 6:24; Lk 18:18–23; Acts 19:21–41; 1 Cor 8:1–6; Phil 3:18–19; Col 3:5; 1 Jn 5:20–21.
Line 70	Gen 41:1–45; Ruth 1–4; 1 Kings 12:1–20; Jer 36; Zeph 3:1–2; Mt 15:21–28; Mk 5:15–20; 9:38–41; 16:9–11; Lk 7:36–50; 10:30–35; Jn 4:27–30, 39; 20:11–18; Acts 24; 1 Cor 14:33b–35; 1 Tim 2:11–12.
Line 71	Lev 25:25–55; Deut 15:1–11; Ps 34:14; 72:1–4, 12–14; Is 58; Amos 5:11–24; Mic 6:6–8; Mt 5:9; 25:31–46; Rom 14:17–19; Gal 5:13–26; Heb 12:14; 13:1–3, 20–21; Jas 1:22–2:26.
Confessions	SC, XIII, XIV, XXIV; HC, qq 86–129; SHC, IV, XVII, XXIII, XXX; WCF, IX, XII, XIX–XXIII, XXV, XXXIV, 3, XXXV; WSC, qq 35, 36, 98–107; WLC, qq 75, 76, 91–148; BD, II; C67, IB, IIA1, 3, 4, IIB2.
72–76	Scripture
Lines 72–74	Lev 19:1–4; Neh 7:73b–8:12; Ps 68:32–35; 96; 100; Mt 13:44; Lk 9:23; 24:44–53; Jn 15:10–11; Acts 1:8, 13:52; Rom 7:4–6; 12:1–3, 9–21; 15:13; 1 Cor 3:16–17; 13; 2 Cor 1:12; Eph 1:3–2:21; 1 Thess 1:4–8; 5:16–18; 1 Pet 1:13–16.
Lines 75–76	Is 65:17; 66:22–23; Mt 24:42–44; 25:1–13; Mk 13:32–37; Lk 14:15–24; 1

Cor 15:51–58; 16:21–24; 2 Pet 3; *Rev 21:1–22:5; 22:20.*

Confessions   HC, qq 31, 32, 86 and all of Part III; SHC, XIV, XVI, XXIX; WCF, VII, 5, XIII–XVI, XIX, XXI–XXIV, XXXIV; WSC, qq 39–82; WLC, qq 56, 175; BD, II, 2; C67, IB, IC1, IIA, III.

Lines 77–80

77–80   Scripture   Ps 27:1–10; 91; 118:1–6; 139:1–18; Is 25:6–9; Jn 3:16; *Rom 8:31–39;* Eph 2:1–10; 2 Tim 2:8–13; Jas 1:12; 1 Pet 1:3–9; 1 Jn 4:7–21.

Confessions   NC, 3rd art.; AC, 3rd art.; SC, XVI, XVII; HC, qq 1, 50–58; SHC, XXVI; WCF, XVII, XVIII; WLC, qq 67, 196; BD, II, 2; C67, IB, IC, ICI, III.

Trust in the Triune God

1. To Whom We Belong
(Lines 1–6)

```
1      In life and in death we belong to God.
2         Through the grace of our Lord Jesus Christ,
3            the love of God,
4               and the communion of the Holy Spirit,
5      we trust in the one triune God, the Holy One of Israel,
6            whom alone we worship and serve.
```

In life and in death we belong to God. This terse beginning announces the good news about our relationship to God, whatever our condition. This claim stands in sharp contrast to the nagging fear that we may be lost in an impersonal cosmos. It also stands in sharp contrast to the sense that the conflicting loyalties of our pluralistic world are so great that nothing is ultimately worth living for or dying for. This bold assertion of faith specifies our identity no matter what. It does more than say where life and death are to be found. It says where *we* are to be found in life and in death—belonging to God. The rest of the Brief Statement of Faith unfolds and clarifies the implications of this central conviction of the gospel.

The assurance of belonging to God redefines other meanings of belonging. What ties us to God, what in fact makes a scattering of individuals into a people who think of themselves as God's, is God's covenanting initiative that reaches out to them in love. In the face of everything that leads men and women to devalue themselves and others, in the face of every kind of obviously pulverizing adversity, God continues to disclose God's self as creator and carer and deliverer. The appropriate response, in all its forms, is one of giving praise for this particular belonging. That is the main reason for the prominence given to the "Old Hundredth" in Reformed worship, thought, and ethics:

> Make a joyful noise to the Lord, all the earth!
> Worship the Lord with gladness;
>> come into his presence with singing.
> Know that the Lord is God.
>> It is he that made us, and we are his;
>> we are his people, and the sheep of his pasture.
> Enter his gates with thanksgiving,
>> and his courts with praise.
>> Give thanks to him, bless his name.
> For the Lord is good;
>> his steadfast love endures forever,
>> and his faithfulness to all generations.
>
> (Ps. 100)

Such joyful belonging alters the way persons relate to the whole of creation, the way we act and the reasons for which we act. The acting out of this joyful belonging is the ethics of the people of God, a freedom *from* being possessed by others or being possessed by self and a freedom *to* be for others and self. This is what the Barmen Declaration refers to as being delivered "from the godless fetters of this world for a free, grateful service of God's creatures" (*Book of Confessions* 8.14). It is one of the most striking features of the Christian life as dedicated, consecrated to God. In Calvin's eloquent words:

> We are not our own: let us therefore not set it as our goal to seek what is expedient for us according to the flesh. We are not our own: in so far as we can, let us therefore forget ourselves and all that is ours. Conversely, we are God's: let us therefore live for him and die for him. We are God's: let his wisdom and will therefore rule all our actions. We are God's: let all the parts of our life accordingly strive toward him as our only lawful goal. (*Institutes* 3.7.1)

Acknowledging that we belong to God is an act of praise and an ethical commitment. It is also a source of comfort.

Behind this first line of the Brief Statement of Faith one can hear the classic opening of the Heidelberg Catechism:

Q. 1. What is your only comfort, in life and in death?

A. That I belong—body and soul, in life and in death—not to myself but to my faithful Savior, Jesus Christ, who at the cost of his own blood has fully paid for all my sins and has completely freed me from the dominion of the devil; that he protects me so well that without the will of my Father in heaven not a hair can fall from my head; indeed, that everything must fit his purpose for my salvation. Therefore, by his Holy Spirit, he also assures me of eternal life, and makes me wholeheartedly willing and ready from now on to live for him. (4.001)

That passage touches on many themes that will deserve discussion in connection with later sections of the Brief Statement. Here there are two things to note. First, the "comfort" to which the Heidelberg Catechism refers is an active assurance of God's mercy, for which we express our gratitude in wholehearted and willing service. Second, that reference to "comfort" makes God's providence fervently personal, in a way that captures Jesus' assurances about God's care for each of us.

That personal tone is also a distinctive characteristic of the Heidelberg Catechism: the faith it teaches is not an abstract set of beliefs that applies only to others, but saving faith which is true for *me* and *my* condition. Such personal emphasis, however, also appears in many of the other documents of the Reformation. Luther's Smaller Catechism reflects it too, in speaking of Christ's forgiveness: "In this Christian church he daily and abundantly forgives all my sins, and the sins of all believers, and on the last day he will raise me and all the dead and will grant eternal life to me and to all who believe in Christ. This is most certainly true."[1]

Through the grace of our Lord Jesus Christ, the love of God, and the communion of the Holy Spirit, we trust in the one triune God, the Holy One of Israel, whom alone we worship and serve. This is a complex sentence whose meaning is best understood when we observe its structure. The hinge is the statement "we trust in the one triune God." The qualifying phrases preceding this hinge specify *how this trust comes about*. The qualifying words and clause that follow the hinge specify, even more, *the focus of this trust*.

Trust in the one triune God comes about *through the grace of our Lord Jesus Christ, the love of God, and the communion of the Holy Spirit*. This formulation is taken from the apostolic benediction as it appears in 2 Corinthians 13:13 (v.14 in the RSV). The Brief Statement of Faith follows its order, beginning with Jesus Christ (lines 7–26) before turning to the traditional "first Person" of the Trinity (lines 27–51) and then to the Holy Spirit (lines 52–76). Throughout the centuries, summaries of the faith being confessed have been differently arranged. The most widely used order is that of the Nicene and Apostles' creeds, namely what the church believes concerning God the "Father" first, then the "Son," and then the "Holy Spirit." The main thing about either ordering is that the content of each section of the confession is presupposed in the other parts and reinforces them, and no part would be intelligible without reference to the others. Each of the sections refers to material more fully dealt with elsewhere—whether the order be that of the Nicene Creed or the one used here. That is also why the opening section (lines 1–6) and the closing section (lines 77–80) are important to use even when a congregation uses only one of the three middle sections in a given service of worship (see the Suggestions for Use in Liturgy and Teaching): we need to affirm that our trust is always in the one triune God, not somehow in some exclusive work of one of the three Persons.

The apostolic benediction particularly recommends itself as a starting point and organizing principle for a statement of faith at this time in the church's experience, for two main reasons.

First, it corresponds to a common experiential order of coming to know and identify the God in whom we believe as the triune God. Time and time again persons look back at the path by which they came to love and trust God and find that it was from experiencing deliverance from sin and freedom for new life that they, then, came to trust the goodness of creation.

Even those who take it for granted that creation is beautiful and good are sometimes unaware of what an ambitious interpretation must be involved in that judgment unless one simply shuts one's eyes to much evidence in the opposite direction. Not all of life can be forced into any scheme in which everything already makes sense. It is false marketing of the gospel to suggest that if people who are racked with pain and caught in the quicksands of futility only believed enough, the goodness behind it all would be apparent. What is true—and this is the grace sufficient for joyful perseverance—is the fact of God's love manifest through Christ by the power of the Holy Spirit. This is what assures believers that they belong to a loving God, to whom all creation belongs.

It seems appropriate, therefore, to begin a confession with our trust in Jesus Christ, who gave "his life for the sins of the world" (line 22) and the God who "raised this Jesus from the dead, . . . breaking the power of sin and evil, delivering us from death to life eternal" (lines 23, 25–26), before turning to affirm that "in sovereign love God created the world good" (line 29). The apostolic benediction follows just that order, beginning with "the grace of the Lord Jesus Christ."

Second, the language of the apostolic benediction provides the room necessary to the church today to confess our faith in the one triune God and to do so in ways that are more inclusive than simply repeating the formula of "Father, Son, and Holy Spirit." That language still appears in the Doxology which is sung or said at the end of the Brief Statement. It is part of the baptismal formula, whose use is one of the major ways Presbyterians continue to be united with other branches of the Christian community, in a world whose fragmentation makes such a shared faith all the more essential. Just to repeat that formula, however, in the face of the need to reconfess the faith today would be to say less than the doctrine which that formula was, and is, intended to serve—namely, to celebrate the identity of the God who calls us to be God's people in successive generations and in shifting cultural contexts. That is why images that also liken God to a mother (line 49) are so important in this Brief Statement of Faith. That is also why the image of God is inclusively described, as it is in lines 29–32, why Sarah is given equal billing with Abraham as recipient of the covenant, and why the stand on the inclusiveness of all ministries of the church is taken in line 64. The shape and contents of each section, and the ordering of the sections, are consciously constructed to bring out the dynamic character of the Trinitarian faith—really, the faith in the triune God—being confessed in each section.

In each section, we confess faith in the triune God. That is, it is the triune God who is the creator, the triune God who is the redeemer, the triune God who is the sanctifier. The Brief Statement of Faith presupposes and builds on what earlier documents in the *Book of Confessions* teach about God. From them it is clear that the mystery being confessed is that God is eternally triune, is triune prior to God's actions beyond God's self, is triune prior to the functions of creating, redeeming, and sanctifying. That creation exists, that creation is redeemed, and that life is sanctified are the results of who God is eternally. The threeness-in-unity is certainly not reducible to three functions or three modes of revelation. The church has always had firmly to resist reducing the three Persons—the three ways God is eternally one God—to three functions. Therefore we cannot simply identify "Creator," "Redeemer," and "Sanctifier" as the names of the three Persons of the Trinity.

The action of the 197th (1985) General Assembly was careful and balanced on this matter. It acknowledged the need to expand and recover the range of ways of speaking of God, especially ways that countered a certain gender prejudice which cannot be denied. Yet it rightly said:

> The Trinitarian designation, "Father-Son-Holy Spirit," is an ancient creedal formula and as such should not be altered. It is deeply rooted in our theological tradition, is shared widely by the church catholic, and is basic to many of our ecumenical relationships. It is not theologically acceptable to refer to the persons of the Trinity in terms of function alone. . . . While the language of the Trinitarian formula should remain unchanged, we must still remember that this formula is not the only way by which we refer to God, and that efforts to express the fullness of our knowledge in terms of being and function are to be encouraged.[2]

Introducing our faith in the triune God with Paul's language—"the grace of our Lord Jesus Christ, the love of God, and the communion of the Holy Spirit"—provides an appropriate and biblical formula that avoids the exclusively male language of "Father" and "Son," yet does not divide up God's work among the different Persons of the Trinity.

The one God is not divisible into the works of creation, redemption, and sanctification; the same God is at work in all and each. That is the first and essential thing to be remembered when the church reconfesses its faith in the triune God. Once that is firmly held to, we have to go on to make a complementary statement, namely, that certain experiences of God's being for us and for the rest of creation are considered in connection with one of the ways of God's being eternally (one of the eternal "Persons") more than with the others. Hence, creation is not the exclusive work of the One whom Jesus called Father. Jesus is the incarnation of the eternal Word by whom all things were made, and the Holy Spirit is confessed to be the Lord and Life-giver. Still, traditionally most of the church's teaching about creation and providence is located in the article of the creed that deals mainly with the first Person of the Trinity. So it is with redemption and sanctification. Redemption is not exclusively the work of Jesus the incarnate Word, nor sanctification exclusively the work of the Holy Spirit. Still, the bulk of the church's teaching about those realities is located respectively in the articles of the creed dealing with the eternal Word, or Son, of God and with the Holy Spirit.

These are matters of the deepest importance to the wholeness of the experience of the gospel, not peripheral technicalities. That is emphasized by the choice of the word "trust" in describing what it is we are brought to through the grace of our Lord Jesus Christ, the love of God, and the fellowship of the Holy Spirit: *we trust in the one triune God, the Holy One of Israel, whom alone we worship and serve.* That God encounters us in these ways, moves us to respond to God's self in these ways, evokes from us a knowing commitment, a covenanting response, an adoring delight in the goodness of the Subject who encounters us. Such trust includes the commitment to worship and serve only this, the true, God. So important is the identity of this trust to which we are moved by God's initiative that it becomes the opening statement for each of the following sections of the Brief Statement of Faith: *We trust in Jesus Christ, fully human, fully God* (lines 7–8); *We trust in God, whom Jesus called Abba, Father* (lines 27–28); and *We trust in God the Holy Spirit, everywhere the giver and renewer of life* (lines 52–53). God is not some commodity to be used, no matter what ends we may, at the moment, judge to be most worthwhile. Nor is God some data base to be accessed, or some body of knowledge to be mastered enough to be useful. The benefits of knowing God are indeed lavishly bestowed; but they come only as by-products, as it were, of focusing on the One thus known and with the kind of knowing that Subject engenders.

The Reformed tradition has been particularly fond of describing that knowledge as "affective knowledge," or "knowledge of the heart," or that knowledge which belongs to "piety." It is the kind of knowing that involves the whole person, the emotions no less than the intellect, the senses no less than thoughts, devotion no less than deduction. That is what lies behind the assertion that the triune God is a mystery to be adored with our whole being. That is quite different, incidentally, from the anti-intellectualism that throws up its hands when it comes to the central mystery of the faith and says it is all incomprehensible and abstract. The mystery of the Trinity is adored as mystery, not because of ignorance or abstraction, but from wonderment, awe, marvel in the face of the magnitude and specificity and freshness of God's grace which brings us into the fellowship God wills to have with others. Calvin had a special predilection for treating the mystery of the Trinity this way. He says:

> Yet the greatness of the mystery warns us how much reverence and sobriety we ought to use in investigating this. And that passage in Gregory of Nazianzus vastly delights me: "I cannot think on the one without quickly being encircled by the splendor of the three; nor can I discern the three without being straightway carried back to the one." Let us not, then, be led to imagine a trinity of persons that keeps our thoughts distracted and does not at once lead them back to that unity. Indeed, the words "Father," "Son," and "Spirit" imply a real distinction—let no

one think that these titles, whereby God is variously designated from his works, are empty—but a distinction, not a division.[3]

The triune God is confessed in lines 5 and 6 to be the *Holy One of Israel, whom alone we worship and serve.* This specification contains an important affirmation, and is open to considerable misunderstanding.

The misunderstanding to which it is open is that for Israel to be Israel, it must acknowledge the Holy One to be the triune God. A variation of this misunderstanding is that if one only looks carefully enough, the doctrine of the Trinity is somehow taught in the Old Testament—or, for that matter, is explicitly taught in the New Testament. In fact, however, it is the church that confesses Jesus to be the promised Anointed One (that is what "Christ" means) for whom the faithful remnant of Israel looks. It is the church that confesses that the God who is witnessed to in the accounts of the New Testament is the same God who is witnessed to by the people of the Old Testament. It is the church that confesses the triune God.

Nevertheless, the Brief Statement affirms that the One whom the church knows to be the triune God is not one god among many: the God the church confesses is the God known in Old and New Testaments. The true, living God is not partly god, of this region or of this activity or of this people but not of that region or activity or people. Such a partly god would not be God. The struggle toward monotheism is still evident in the writings of the Old Testament; but, whether one reads it back into earlier narratives or not, Israel came to believe that the God whose deliverance they actively remember is the one true God over all the earth and over all the peoples. This is what they affirmed in the great Shema, Israel's constitutive cry of faith: "Hear, O Israel: The Lord is our God, the Lord alone. You shall love the Lord your God with all your heart, and with all your soul, and with all your might" (Deut. 6:4–5; the term "Shema" comes from the Hebrew word "hear," with which the formula begins).

The implications of there being one God over all the earth and over all the peoples is the material of Israel's struggle over what it means to belong to this God. Israel confesses God to be one and over all things, not just when events take a felicitous turn for Israel. Israel also (perhaps especially) confesses God to be one when God's benevolent ways seem devastatingly hidden, as with the experience of captivity. The earliest Christian community read and sang and taught the writings of what would come to be known as the Old Testament as applying to itself. The things that had taken place with the coming of Jesus the Christ, his teachings and death and resurrection, and the coming upon many of the Holy Spirit—these things occurred, according to the earliest Christian community, in order that what was written might be fulfilled. That meant above all that God was faithful to God's covenant purposes, that what the church experiences is what Israel also experienced, namely, the covenant steadfastness of the one true God.

The confession that God is one, and is the same one witnessed to by the communities whose memories shaped the Old and the New Testaments, has an unmistakable ethical bite to it. That God is one and steadfastly faithful means that God's people are not to go after the pretend gods, the idols. Idols are, of course, far more than just graven images of alternative deities. Idols are the persons or things or ideals or memories or self-images or failures, and so on, to which we so cling that life would not be worth living without them. Idols come in all sizes and shapes, and their power consists precisely in their not appearing to be "idols" but rather appearing to be the most successful procurers of those things dearest to their followers' hearts. The most attractive of idols commend themselves by the modesty of the claims they appear to make on our lives—attending to this one counts only for success or happiness or justice or whatever, in just this section of life or just this part of experience. The idols flourish by compromise, and invite the division of worship and praise—a compromise and division we call polytheism.

Over against the convenience of polytheism, it is an act of daring faith to assert that the one triune God is the Holy One of Israel, *whom alone we worship and serve*. This is simply an absurd claim, of course, if taken apart from God's grace, love, and communion, which quicken and shape trust. None of us has the capacity to turn away from all idols, to worship and serve God alone. Taken, however, as a description of who we are in response to who God is, then this claim is a pledge, a covenant commitment which is daily, hourly renewed. The *alone* is crucial to this pledge, and is a favorite word in some of the strongest Reformed confessions. It is implied in the first of the Barmen Declaration's evangelical truths: "Jesus Christ, as he is attested for us in Holy Scripture, is the one Word of God which we have to hear and which we have to trust and obey in life and in death" (8.11). And it resounds in the beginning chapter of the Scots Confession, the section that deals with the same thing as the opening line of the Brief Statement of Faith, the triune God in whom we put our trust:

> We confess and acknowledge one God alone, to whom we must cleave, whom alone we must serve, whom alone we must worship, and in whom alone we must put our trust; who is eternal, infinite, immeasurable, incomprehensible, omnipotent, invisible; one in substance and yet distinct in three persons, the Father, the Son, and the Holy Ghost. (3.01)

Part of what is at stake in the question of idolatry is the honor due God alone, but that is only part of it. In fact, God is most honored by God's people choosing the life that God freely offers and wills for them. The most obvious difference between the idols and God is that God is a living Subject in whose service one finds life, whereas the idols are dead things, the service of which is a deadly business. That is the way the great choice confronting Israel in Deuteronomy 30 is put: "I have set before you life and death, blessings and curses. Choose life so that you and your descendants may live, loving the Lord your God, obeying him, and holding fast to him" (vs. 19–20). It is also the way the psalmist draws the contrast and corresponding ethical implications in Psalm 115:

> Their idols are silver and gold,
>   the work of human hands.
> They have mouths, but do not speak;
>   eyes, but do not see.
> They have ears, but do not hear;
>   noses, but do not smell.
> They have hands, but do not feel;

feet, but do not walk;
they make no sound in their throats.
Those who make them are like them;
so are all who trust in them.
O Israel, trust in the Lord!

(Vs. 4–9)

"Those who make them are like them;/so are all who trust in them./O Israel, trust in the Lord!" There you have it, the connection between where we put our trust and what sort of persons or things we become. Knowing that we belong to the living God entails certain realities which are to be reconfessed, in word and action. Such active, critical reconfession is continually refocused as believers are moved to trust and obey, in life and in death, the one Word who is Jesus Christ as he is attested to in the scriptures. After this introduction, the Brief Statement of Faith turns to the section that most deals with him.

Trust in Jesus Christ,
Fully Human, Fully God

2. Incarnation
(Lines 7–8)

7   We trust in Jesus Christ
8   fully human, fully God.

We trust in Jesus Christ, fully human, fully God. These few words contain the scandal of the gospel. Israel and the church are commanded to put their trust in *none other than God.* Should they then trust in Jesus Christ? That question goes to the very heart of the good news that Jesus proclaimed, the good news of what was being inaugurated with his coming. He is not just the proclaimer of the good news—his identity as "the coming one" for which Israel looked is part of the proclamation.

In Luke's Gospel, for example, John the Baptizer, arrested and in prison, hearing of Jesus' great works, sends his disciples to Jesus with the question, "Are you the one who is to come, or are we to wait for another?" Jesus' reply is a shocking announcement of good news, because he connects his ministry with the figure promised in Isaiah: "Go and tell John what you have seen and heard: the blind receive their sight, the lame walk, the lepers are cleansed, the deaf hear, the dead are raised, the poor have good news brought to them. And blessed is anyone who takes no offense at me" (Luke 7:22–23; the reference is to Isa. 29:18–19; 35:5–6; and 61:1).

Jesus' deeds and teachings broke into people's lives with enormous hope, with actual changes in their most evident and immediate conditions. Even more important, however, the individual deeds and teachings were signs of a fundamental change in the reality of the world. The final days were at hand, and God's long-awaited, new form of ruling was being ushered in with the coming of Jesus the Christ. It is important to get this straight. The reign of God, the new aeon, was not brought about as a result of the individual miracles; the actuality of the new reign of God was breaking in, and the miracles were signs of that fact. The choice facing people now, as then, is whether or not they awaken to that reality and change their lives to adjust to it—whether or not they repent and believe the good news.

The message and the repentance for which it calls are so radical because it is the rule of *God* that the Christ, Jesus, claims to usher in. That raises the fundamental question behind the conflict that eventually took Jesus to the cross: Did he or did he not blaspheme, not just with what he said, but in the things he did and the authority with which he did them? Over and over again, the accounts of his ministry show his opponents convinced that he could not be the Messiah because he did not strictly follow the interpretations of the Law as they had by then received and interpreted it. Where his opponents see him only to be breaking the Law, the Gospels present Jesus as reaching back to observe the Law at a far more fundamental level, and so to be fulfilling the purposes for which it had been given.

A passage that catches up these themes is the one, again from Luke, in which Jesus encounters a paralytic whose friends tear a hole in the roof so they can lower his stretcher before Jesus. The dramatic juxtaposition is startling, for the account says that when Jesus saw the faith of these friends, he addressed the one who was paralyzed:

> "Friend, your sins are forgiven you." Then the scribes and the Pharisees began to question, "Who is this who is speaking blasphemies? Who can forgive sins but God alone?" When Jesus perceived their questionings, he answered them, "Why do you raise such questions in your hearts? Which is easier, to say, 'Your sins are forgiven you,' or to say, 'Stand up and walk'? But so that you may know that the Son of Man has authority on earth to forgive sins"—he said to the one who was paralyzed—"I say to you, stand up and take your bed and go to your home." Immediately he stood up before them, took what he had been lying on, and went to his home, glorifying God. Amazement seized all of them,

and they glorified God and were filled with awe, saying, "We
have seen strange things today." (Luke 5:20–26)

This passage needs no interrupting comment because it is
clear enough in its own dramatic impact and pace. Moreover,
the account that immediately follows heightens even further
the issue at stake. Jesus goes out from this incident and sees a
tax collector, Levi, who is sitting at the tax office. Jesus tells
Levi to follow him, and he leaves everything and does so. Then
he, Levi, puts on a big feast at which Jesus and his disciples sit
down at table with a "large crowd of tax collectors."

> The Pharisees and their scribes were complaining to his disci-
> ples, saying, "Why do you eat and drink with tax collectors and
> sinners?" Jesus answered, "Those who are well have no need of
> a physician, but those who are sick; I have come to call not the
> righteous but sinners to repentance." (Luke 5:30–32)

The healing of the paralytic shows the closest possible connection between forgiveness of sins and wholeness. It also
shows that forgiveness and healing for all the people is at hand
with the coming of this one, Jesus, who is the Son of Man, the
mysterious figure the prophet Daniel had predicted would
come with clouds of heaven to establish a reign that will "never
be destroyed" (Dan. 7:13–14)—who has, indeed, the power to
forgive sins. Jesus' opponents are correct in their premise,
namely, that God alone can forgive sins, but not in their conclusion. They draw the wrong conclusion because they reason
that someone who comports with sinners, who eats with tax
collectors (the Roman occupiers' corrupt toadies), who heals
on the Sabbath, cannot be the long-awaited Messiah. They recognize that he is a popular inspirer of the masses, a clever
teacher, and, unmistakably, an awesome wonder-worker. He
might even be a true prophet. The only question is whether he
is indeed the figure variously entitled "the Coming One," "the
Son of Man," or, most comprehensively, "the Anointed One"
(which is what "Messiah" and "Christ" mean), who ushers in
the final times in which God's promises to Israel will be fulfilled and every nation will look to Zion for its justice and
wholeness.

Jesus' opponents were not mean-spirited persons who simply disliked him. They ardently looked for the vindication of God's justice, and they were outraged that it should be thought to be accurately portrayed by the goings-on engendered by Jesus' deeds and teachings. We need to get clear on their motives for more reasons than simply historical interest: for his opponents then acted from a sense of revulsion, even outrage, at God's ways—which people throughout the centuries, and including each of us, share—a sense of outrage at calling this "justice." Jesus' identification with the Servant of the Lord in Isaiah, the conflicts that claim set in motion with those determined that the Messiah should fit other criteria, Jesus' obedience to the One who sent him—these led to the cross.

It is a scandal to confess that this person, whom Mary delivered in a stable of a provincial town, is vindicated as the Lord of all and the one by whom all things were made. More of that scandal presently. For now, we must not miss the prior scandal, which is that of confessing that Jesus is the Christ whose obedience to the One who sent him leads to the cross. That is the reason for the startling reversal in Jesus' treatment of Peter in the account Matthew gives of his confession.

Jesus asks the disciples, "Who do people say that the Son of Man is?" (Matt. 16:13). The disciples reply, "Some say John the Baptist, but others Elijah, and still others Jeremiah or one of the prophets" (v. 14). So far the question has remained ambiguous and possibly abstract—it might refer to interpretations about the general expectation of the "Son of Man" and not apply to Jesus himself at all. That makes all the sharper the question Jesus then puts to the disciples: "But who do you say that I am?" Now the disciples are confronted by an even more decisive question: How is it that Jesus fits in this presupposed general expectation of the Son of Man?

> Simon Peter answered, "You are the Messiah, the Son of the living God." And Jesus answered him, "Blessed are you, Simon son of Jonah! For flesh and blood has not revealed this to you, but my Father in heaven. And I tell you, you are Peter, and on this rock [*petra*] I will build my church, and the gates of Hades will not prevail against it. I will give you the keys of the kingdom of heaven, and whatever you bind on earth will be bound in

heaven, and whatever you loose on earth will be loosed in heaven." Then he sternly ordered the disciples not to tell anyone that he was the Messiah. (Vs. 16–20)

It is impossible to miss the sharp contrast Jesus uses when he replies to Peter's answer. Jesus says that Peter's answer is not what he could have gotten from flesh and blood, which is what both the people's answers and the disciples' answers are founded on. Peter's answer comes by way of revelation.

This passage of scripture is one of the most influential and controversial in the history of the church. For the moment, we can leave aside what is meant by the power of the keys and what the "*petra*" (rock) is on which the church is founded. These matters will be taken up again in the third section of the Brief Statement of Faith. Now, though, we must note the inseparability presented here of two things: confessing Jesus to be "the Messiah, the Son of the living God," and belonging to the community of costly discipleship. The question "But you, who do you say that I am?" confronts a person with a crisis and makes a decision unavoidable. It is a crisis over whether or not the final days are at hand, over whether or not Jesus is the one expected to usher in those final days, and over whether or not to repent and believe the good news.

At the same time, the decision about Jesus' identity is a decision about the community to which one belongs. Following Jesus the Christ entails membership in the community whose ultimate loyalties include the cross. That dimension of the crisis is vividly put in the verses that immediately follow Peter's being blessed for what was revealed to him. He made the confession, but he was clearly unaware of its implications for Jesus' destiny and the destiny of those who follow Jesus:

From that time on, Jesus began to show his disciples that he must go to Jerusalem and undergo great suffering at the hands of the elders and chief priests and scribes, and be killed, and on the third day be raised. And Peter took him aside and began to rebuke him, saying, "God forbid it, Lord! This must never happen to you." But he turned and said to Peter, "Get behind me, Satan! You are a stumbling block to me; for you are setting your mind not on divine things but on human things."

Then Jesus told his disciples, "If any want to become my followers, let them deny themselves and take up their cross and follow me. For those who want to save their life will lose it, and those who lose their life for my sake will find it." (Vs. 21–25)

The cross, whether Jesus' or the disciples' after him, is not the final word. Losing one's life for Christ's sake is not even the final word. The cross and losing one's life, even for Christ's sake, are not ends in themselves. For Christ came that people may have life—not death—more abundantly. It is just that there is no bypassing the costly obedience, which paradoxically is what issues forth in joyful deliverance. It is just that the quality of the new, abundant life is redefined by sharing in Christ's death and resurrection. It is just that baptism into newness of life leads to sharing in the shape and consequences of Jesus' own ministry, that of the Servant Lord who is vindicated as the Christ by the resurrection. The cross in question here is, after all, not just one of the many gibbets used to maintain Roman law and order so efficiently. It is *that* cross, the cross on which was crucified the One who was raised from the dead. The saving identity is that the one who was crucified is the one who was raised. In Acts, when Peter heals a crippled beggar at the city gate "in the name of Jesus Christ of Nazareth" (Acts 3:6), he explains that the one who was crucified is "the Author of life, whom God raised from the dead" (3:15; see also 2:22–24 and 4:7–12).

There is, then, an inevitable connection between confessing Jesus to be the Christ and belonging to the community that follows him to the cross and beyond. We need now, however, to take another look at the full form of Peter's confession, "You are the Messiah, the Son of the living God." Matthew presents the claim and designation as decisive in identifying who Jesus is, and also in identifying who the living God is. "Son of the living God" says something about the uniqueness of Jesus the Christ; but it also says something about the nature of the living God—especially when the rest of the passage goes on to indicate that the saving way of this God is through the cross, to victory over death.

This is important to keep in mind when we turn to consider what it means for the church to confess the mystery of the incarnation, namely, that this Jesus Christ is "truly God, truly human, one person."[1] Otherwise the whole matter gets couched in terms of how much "divinity" there is to Jesus (or in what ways he was divine), with the "divinity" or the "divine" being defined before we take account of, and quite separated from, what we know of God from the cross of the risen Lord. The same is true of Christ's humanity: the whole matter could be (and often is) reduced to speculating about how much "humanity" there was to Jesus (or in what ways he was human), with the meanings of those terms treated as if they were self-evident or self-explanatory. As Christians, however, we deny that one can know what divinity or humanity is in abstraction, apart from the concrete life and death and resurrection of this Jesus of Nazareth.

The church confesses Jesus to be the Christ, one person, truly God, truly human. In reconfessing the full humanity and full divinity of the one Person, Jesus Christ, the Brief Statement of Faith is aligning itself with the Reformed confessions on this particular, essential tenet of the faith. The ancient and modern Reformed documents in the Presbyterian *Book of Confessions* are unwavering on this point, as—not incidentally—are the new confessions of Reformed churches around the world today. The sixteenth- and seventeenth-century Reformed confessions made, as part of the content of their new confession, the point that they stood together with the ancient ecumenical councils on this matter. The same is true with the Barmen Declaration and the Confession of 1967.

The Brief Statement of Faith reverses the usual order, and affirms the identity of Jesus Christ, "fully human, fully God." It does so not to deny the mystery of the incarnation, but to take a strong stand on what is perhaps too readily minimized today: the full *humanity* of Jesus Christ. And it uses the adverb "fully" to modify both "human" and "God," to guard against—an ancient as well as a modern error—one of the ways of watering down the saving mystery. That watering down says, Yes, Jesus is really or truly divine and really or truly human, but only in the sense that he is partly the one and partly the other. When we confess that Jesus is "fully human, fully God," however, the church is confessing the unity of God and humanity in this one Person, Jesus Christ.

Jesus Christ is *fully human, fully God*. That confession is an explication of what it means for the whole inhabited earth, indeed for the whole of creation, that this Jesus—crucified, dead, and buried, and on the third day risen from the dead—is the Lord and Savior of the world, not just the Anointed One of Israel. The actual formulas in which that confession was worked out belong to developments culminating in the language of the great councils of the church in the fourth and fifth centuries; but the fundamental fact of which the subsequent language takes account is already witnessed to in the New Testament.

That fundamental fact is that the end times, which were ushered in by Jesus as the Christ, included the outpouring of the Holy Spirit on other peoples besides Israel. At first, at Pentecost, this outpouring was on Jews returning from all over the world to Jerusalem, who spoke the languages of the countries in which they had settled. Subsequently, though, the earliest church council (at Jerusalem) had to deal with the implications of the fact that Gentiles were also recipients of the promises of God made to Israel. They too were receiving the Holy Spirit and were believing the gospel; and the question was whether they too were to be baptized. By deciding in the affirmative, the earliest church was making a claim, taking a confessing stand, about the extent of God's inclusive purposes through the person and work of Jesus the Christ. That decision shaped both the choice of the books to be included in the New Testament and the choice of creedal language to affirm the identity of the God behind creation and redemption.

One of the marks of the books included in the New Testament is their affirmation of the continuity between the promises of the Old Testament and the wholeness witnessed to in the New. This affirmation carried with it the confession that the one God, to whom the whole of creation belongs, is the active Subject also of the events witnessed to in the New Testament—that is, the God of the New Testament is not another God, the redeemer instead of the creator. The books chosen to be the New Testament proclaim that the one God whom Israel already experienced as creator and deliverer fulfills the purposes of the covenanting promises by the events witnessed and proclaimed by the earliest church. That is the confession, for example, at the beginning of The Letter to the Hebrews:

> Long ago God spoke to our ancestors in many and various ways by the prophets, but in these last days he has spoken to us by a Son, whom he appointed heir of all things, through whom he also created the worlds. He is the reflection of God's glory and the exact imprint of God's very being, and he sustains all things by his powerful word. (Heb. 1:1–3; see also Eph. 1:3–10; 2 Cor. 3:12–4:15; and the prologue to John's Gospel)

There is a precision of language, a leanness of formulation, to the church's subsequent creedal language on this point. The church, ancient or modern, is not saying more in order to add to the apostolic teaching and preaching. It is saying what must be said in the context of the "whole inhabited earth," in order not to say less than what must be said—and sung, and ethically celebrated—for men and women of all times and places to hear the good news that the Jewish Messiah, Jesus of Nazareth, is the mediator of wholeness, in creation and in redemption, for them and for everyone else. The precision, the economy of what is liturgically and doctrinally and ethically the ringing truth affectively known, is caught in the piling up of reinforcing imagery in the most ecumenical of the creeds, the "Nicene":

> We believe in one Lord, Jesus Christ, the only Son of God, eternally begotten of the Father, God from God, Light from Light, true God from true God, begotten, not made, of one Being with the Father; through him all things were made. For us and for our salvation he came down from heaven; was incarnate of the Holy Spirit and the Virgin Mary and became truly human. For our sake he was crucified under Pontius Pilate; he suffered death and was buried. On the third day he rose again in accordance with the Scriptures; he ascended into heaven and is seated on the right hand of the Father. He will come again in glory to judge the living and the dead, and his kingdom will have no end.

When churches in cultural contexts subsequent to this reconfess the truth of the incarnation, they are at once taking a stand about at least two things: They are taking a stand about who

Jesus Christ is, and they are taking a stand about the inclusiveness of the catholic (that is, the universal) church as an effective sign of the inclusiveness of God's purposes for the whole human community—and the whole of creation. It is not despite the pluralism of modern society at national and international levels that the reality of the incarnation of the eternal Word of God is reconfessed today. It is exactly because of pluralism, ancient and modern, that the reality of the incarnation is so important to teach, sing about, and respond to in ethical practice. God's saving purposes worked out through the scandalous particularity of Jesus Christ are for all peoples, for all times, for all places. This is the foundation and presupposition of prophetic inclusiveness, the opposite of intolerant exclusiveness. The radical particularity of the eternal Word become flesh as the Jewish Messiah—Jesus of Nazareth, crucified, dead, and buried, risen on the third day, and coming again—is the foundation of an inclusiveness based on criteria of compassionate service, mutual forgiveness, and hope that edifies the other as well as self. That is what the restoration of the image of God, into which all persons are created, is all about: the eternal Word by whom all things were made is the same eternal Word, now enfleshed, by whom all things are made new. Creation and re-creation are held together, and are mutually defining and mutually enriching and mutually correcting, because they are both forms of the inclusive purposes—the loving outgoing of the triune God—which we experience in creation and redemption.

The eternal Word became flesh "for us and for our salvation." The aim and goal of God's living among us as a human is to deliver, restore, and heal the human condition. The incarnation is God's establishing solidarity with humanity, not just to comfort persons, but actively to deliver them. In Calvin's words, it is by the whole course of Christ's obedience that we are made whole (*Institutes* 2.16.5). One of the characteristics of the Brief Statement of Faith is the attention it gives to those things which comprise Christ's activity toward and on behalf of all sorts and conditions of humanity. It is to this that we now turn in the next section.

3. Ministry
(Lines 9–18)

9   Jesus proclaimed the reign of God:
10   preaching good news to the poor
11   and release to the captives,
12   teaching by word and deed
13   and blessing the children,
14   healing the sick
15   and binding up the brokenhearted,
16   eating with outcasts,
17   forgiving sinners,
18   and calling all to repent and believe the gospel.

*Jesus proclaimed the reign of God: preaching . . . teaching . . .
blessing . . . healing . . . binding up . . . eating . . . forgiving . . .
calling . . . .* Lines 9–18 are one sentence, whose central declaration is that Jesus proclaimed the reign of God. His diverse
actions—"preaching," "teaching," "blessing," and so forth—
are the ways that proclamation occurred. These lines also identify those who were the primary recipients of Jesus' eventful
proclamation: *the poor . . . the captives . . . the children . . . the
sick . . . the brokenhearted . . . outcasts . . . sinners . . . all.*

These lines connect what we confess about who Jesus Christ
is (lines 7–8) with what we confess about his death and resurrection (lines 19–26). The order in which this statement treats,
first, Christ's proclamation and then Christ's death and resurrection is part of the content of what is being confessed: the
very nature of what he proclaims and the very dynamics of how

he proclaims it take him to the cross. Christ's ministry is such a fundamental reordering of things, such a radical reversal of existing expectations and priorities, that the proclamation—the presence of the reign of God through this proclaiming Christ—becomes itself a matter of death and life, to Christ himself and those to whom he ministers, to those who oppose him and those who follow him.

The events of Jesus' ministry and its consequences confirmed the fact that Jesus is "the one who is to come" and that God's people are not to "wait for another" (Matt. 11:3; Luke 7:19–20). In treating lines 7 and 8, we have already pointed to the significance of the question John the Baptizer addresses to Jesus from prison when he hears about Jesus' ministry. We need to remember it again here, because the elements of the present section evoke the answer Christ gives to that question by referring to the Anointed One promised in Isaiah. John sends his disciples to ask, "Are you the one who is to come, or are we to wait for another?" "Jesus had just then cured many people of diseases, plagues, and evil spirits, and had given sight to many who were blind. And he answered them [John's disciples], 'Go and tell John what you have seen and heard: the blind receive their sight, the lame walk, the lepers are cleansed, the deaf hear, the dead are raised, the poor have good news brought to them. And blessed is anyone who takes no offense at me.'" (Luke 7:21–23. See also Luke 4:14–21, where Jesus reads the opening of Isaiah 61 and scandalizes those in the synagogue in Nazareth by announcing, "Today this scripture has been fulfilled in your hearing.")

Jesus' reply to John's disciples is not an exhaustive list of the events of his ministry. His response—a composite of elements drawn from what we know as chapters 29, 35, and 61 of Isaiah—is to place those events in the context of a particular tradition of hope, the tradition of prophetic expectation of a coming Messiah. The events confirm the fact that, with what is happening through Jesus' acts and teaching, the promised time of God's deliverance of Israel is at hand. What follows in Luke's account makes it clear that this is the main point. Jesus goes on to put John the Baptizer's own ministry into perspective: John is a prophet:

"Yes, . . . and more than a prophet. This is the one about whom it is written,

> 'See, I am sending my messenger ahead of you,
> who will prepare your way before you.'

I tell you, among those born of women no one is greater than John; yet the least in the kingdom of God is greater than he" (Luke 7:27–28).

Lines 7–8 pointed to one aspect of the announced reign of God: namely, that it is a new aeon, God's timing at the limits of human timing, the inbreaking of God who graciously takes up our time. The lines presently before us call attention to another aspect of the announced reign of God, namely, that it is the inbreaking of God's setting aright things that have gone viciously awry. It is the transforming appearance, the reordering apocalyptic, of *God's* justice. The Brief Statement of Faith rightly uses "reign of God" instead of "kingdom of God" in order to use more inclusive language. Something of the bite, the protesting sharp contrast, gets lost, however, in the absence of "king" or some equivalent personal term hidden in a word like "kingdom," for the principal point of the announced "rule of God" or "dominion of God" or "reign of God" is not what name is used for governance. It is *whose* governance is being announced: the "reign of *God*" is at hand. In the early days of the nation of Israel, the people had sought to have Samuel anoint for them a human king so that they would be like the other nations (1 Sam. 8:5). The Lord said to Samuel, "They have rejected me from being king over them," and Samuel warned the people how a human king would oppress them and their children; but the people persisted. Announcing, as Jesus does, that *God* is the ruler introduces the sharp judgment by which God mercifully does not, after all, let God's people get away with choosing to have another king over them so that they will be like the other nations.

In the reordering of things by this ruler, the Holy One of Israel, those least served by the prevailing human system of justice are exactly the ones whose care is to be preeminent. This new reign is according to God's steadfast love, God's reordering compassion, by which those who are exalted at the expense of others will be brought low and those who have no one to plead their cause will be exalted. Luke makes this quite clear with the hymn from the lips of the one through whose labor the Messiah comes on the scene:

> And Mary said,
> "My soul magnifies the Lord,
>   and my spirit rejoices in God my Savior,
> for he has looked with favor on the lowliness of his servant.
>   Surely, from now on all generations will call me blessed;
> for the Mighty One has done great things for me,
>   and holy is his name.
> His mercy is for those who fear him
>   from generation to generation.
> He has shown strength with his arm;
>   he has scattered the proud in the thoughts of their hearts.
> He has brought down the powerful from their thrones,
>   and lifted up the lowly;
> he has filled the hungry with good things,
>   and sent the rich away empty.
> He has helped his servant Israel,
>   in remembrance of his mercy,
> according to the promise he made to our ancestors,
>   to Abraham and to his descendants forever."
>   (Luke 1:46–55)

This gives a more accurate understanding of what Jesus tells John's disciples they should go back and tell John, in answer to the question of whether or not Jesus is the Coming One. Those who are lifted up for special attention in different descriptions of the Messiah figure in Isaiah are attended to, and what seems like a throwaway or an anticlimax in the message to John heightens the sense of fulfillment: "and the poor have good news brought to them." It is not that the blind and lame and leprous have their immediate needs dealt with, whereas the poor get only a consolation prize. Rather it is that the good news has at its center the announcement that the long-awaited day of the Lord is at hand, when God's justice will be vindicated and in that justice the poor will have preeminent benefits.

For some of the prophets of ancient Israel, the term "the day of the Lord" had an almost technical meaning, and it overlaps into the sense the Gospels convey of the reign of God. In Amos 5:18–24, for example, those who substitute solemn feasts for justice think they know what they are doing when they look for the day of the Lord; but for them it will come as darkness and not as light.

> Take away from me the noise of your songs;
>   I will not listen to the melody of your harps.
> But let justice roll down like waters,
>   and righteousness like an everflowing stream.
> (Vs. 23–24)

Those in special need of justice and righteousness are the ones for whom God's freeing and reordering love has special urgency and priority—those who are least helped by the prevailing definitions and practices of justice, care, acceptance, and health. The prophets' scorn was poured on the worldly wise and wealthy, on those of great power used for themselves and their friends, on those who substitute ritual for justice. The test the prophets use over and over again for justice is how the poor, the oppressed, the strangers and aliens, the sick, the outcast are treated. How they are treated is an index, a symptom, not just of good or bad behavior on the part of the oppressors but of whether the true God is being worshiped—namely, the God who is known as the one who hears the cries of the oppressed and takes action on their behalf, the God who brings into being a people who care for exactly the kind of people whose cry is especially attended to by this God.

It is not that God does not also love the oppressors: God loves them enough not to leave them to their own ways. Nor is it that one can ultimately block the oppressors and the oppressed into permanent categories, ignoring the proclivity of the former oppressed to misuse the benefits of their deliverance. It is just that God's love for all is experienced and identified by the care exercised on behalf of the most needy, who have none to plead their cause. In the individual acts of mercy he performs, in the teaching that calls Israel back to its senses, Christ establishes the justice that is at the same time inseparable from the right worship of God. In and through the ministry of this One, God's justice flows and bears the people along with it in a stream which gathers force so that the presence of God's reign is unmistakable.

The Brief Statement of Faith gives more attention to the individual acts of Christ's ministry than does, for example, either the Apostles' Creed or the Nicene Creed. In those classic documents, the sudden transition from what is confessed concerning the incarnation to what is confessed concerning the death and resurrection is striking. Here, in this document, amplifying on the course of Christ's ministry is no denigration of the reality of the incarnation. In fact, this amplification gives greater specificity to what Calvin considers to be Christ's saving work, namely, "the whole course of his obedience" (*Institutes* 2.16.5). The coming into our human condition, the taking up of our humanity begins, yes, with the incarnation, with the eternal Word becoming flesh—but it continues and its saving significance comes about through the course of Christ's being tested in every way as we are, yet without sin. This emphasis on the whole course of Christ's ministry as being saving is a strong feature in the theology of the second-century bishop Irenaeus, the first great systematic theologian of the church, who put it in terms of Christ's "recapitulating" in himself what it means to live out our lives as God created us to become.[1]

This amplification of Christ's earthly ministry lifts up material that had been minimized in the brevity of the earlier creeds. It points to Christ's actions and teaching as the faithful representative of Israel in God's covenanting purposes. In the place of our inability or refusal to fulfill the covenant, Christ lives through each step of life as God created us to live—and Christ correctly relived, as it were, the course of Israel's testing. In his individual acts of teaching and healing and calling to repentance, Christ is effectively manifesting what God created us to become.

The scope of salvation, or the economy of God's unfolding purposes, the sweep of salvation history as the new Adam is faithful in place of the old Adam—all this indeed is part of what the church confesses. The way that inclusive, saving reality comes to be experienced, remembered, and proclaimed in the

New Testament is through persons' being caught up in the presence and activity of Jesus as the Christ. Their salvation is not procured for them as some sort of transaction effected over their heads or behind their backs. Occurrences "befall them," which so "amaze" them that there can be no returning to business as usual as if those things had not happened. People live and move in radically different directions as a result of the amazing events in which they are caught up. That is what repentance and conversion mean: to change direction, to swing about and face the opposite way, to move forward in a totally different direction. And that is the impact Jesus as the Christ had on the people, the commonest gatherings and most ordinary individuals, among whom Christ lived out his saving ministry.

Christ's effective and correcting compassion is just that: his so loving those among whom he moves that he does what is necessary to heal their diseases, whether of spirit or of body or of relationships. He heals on the Sabbath, thereby making individuals whole, and teaching again the fundamental reason for the commandment to keep the Sabbath holy: as a means of giving our lives a shape and order that will glorify God. (See, for instance, Mark 2:27.) He eats with sinners and thereby gives them public acceptance. They turn away from their former lives and are recalled to *true* righteousness even as the *self*-righteousness of those who look on these "sinners" with contempt is exposed for what it is. Jesus chooses for healing cripples who cannot even move to saving waters; and God's compassion to deliver the most hopeless of conditions is proclaimed. The variety of the conditions is exactly the point: there is no corner of human life that is walled off from the saving presence and activity of God's merciful judgment and judging mercy. People are helped, and helped at the most fundamental level of their perceived and unperceived needs. It is the very heart of the identity of this one as the Christ that he comes as the Servant Lord who redefines what it means both to serve and to be served, to rule and to be ruled.

The concreteness of Christ's ministry—the actual changes he brought about in the most immediate realities of people's lives—is part of his saving significance. One of the most striking features of the accounts of Christ's effects on those around him is that they were amazed, astounded, moved to wonder. It is not merely that people were healed. It is also that their accustomed frameworks of perception were thereby shaken up, were displaced, were stretched in ways previously not imaginable. The ordinary was transformed to such an extent that life in the old pattern was no longer possible. The ordinary tasks and relationships were charged with new signification, new quality as signs themselves of the presence of the new reign of God. The changed lives of persons touched by the Christ became effective signs of the presence of the Coming One.

Just one example of this is the story of Lazarus (John 11 and 12). Of course, the most obvious point about Lazarus is that he was raised from the dead by the one who is the way, the truth, and the life. But that means also that the new life of Lazarus itself becomes a scandalous witness to Christ's identity, so that a price is put on Lazarus' head. The opposition seeks to kill the one just raised from the dead, seeks to undo the new life done him—for the very reason that people who see him alive again are turning to the new life by following Jesus as the Christ.

In John 3, Nicodemus comes to Jesus by night to learn something about his teaching. Jesus says to him, "Very truly, I tell you, no one can see the kingdom of God without being born from above." Nicodemus cannot understand—"How can anyone be born after having grown old?"—and hesitates to commit himself to faith in this new teacher. This business of being born again represents a fundamental challenge to the regime of things-as-they-are. Lazarus alive is a living response to the question Nicodemus asked Jesus in secret.

A distinction used to be made in handbooks of theology between the so-called active obedience of Christ and the so-called passive obedience of Christ. The former usually referred to the acts of his public ministry like teaching, healing, feeding, and so on—the things, in other words, treated in the lines under discussion here. The latter—Christ's so-called passive obedience—on the other hand usually referred to Christ's atoning work on the cross, his obedience unto the death on the cross. Such a distinction, however, rather quickly breaks down. Christ's day-to-day ministry is of a whole cloth with the nature of his ultimate sacrifice. For all the attention given to the trial of Jesus and to speculation about the "last temptation of Christ," the main significance does not have to do with assessing blame. An appalling injustice was done when Christ suffered rejection by his innermost circle, by his closest disciples, as well as by the populace and their leaders, at the same time as the Roman Empire through its representatives abdicated even its own standard of justice.

The stakes, however, are far greater even than is recognized by a debate carried on at that level. At issue is what happens with the inbreaking of the end time, which puts an end to even the very best of human religion and human justice and human promises. The cock crows three times not just before Peter, the shattered rock of commitment among the disciples. The cock crows three times before all ways of carrying on life and work and love and justice according to the old scheme, that which refuses to recognize the presence of God's new reign and to live accordingly. Jesus' daily ministry proclaims and effects the inbreaking of this new reign of God, with the costly compassion that confronts the old order head-on.

4. Cross
(Lines 19–22)

19 Unjustly condemned for blasphemy and sedition,
20 Jesus was crucified,
21   suffering the depths of human pain
22   and giving his life for the sins of the world.

Jesus died on a cross. Even skeptical historians who question nearly everything else in the New Testament concede the historical fact of the crucifixion. The cross has become such a universal Christian symbol, however, that we rarely reflect on its original meaning. We Protestants, who seldom portray the suffering body of Jesus on our crosses, may be particularly inclined to treat the cross as just an abstract mark of Christian faith.

But in the early days of Christianity the cross was obviously shocking and scandalous. The Romans reserved crucifixion for the most despised of criminals—generally escaped slaves, traitors, political rebels. Death on a cross was not only painful, but shameful. Roman citizens, no matter how terrible their crimes, could at least not be crucified.[1] In the Jewish context, too, a cross meant shame and scandal. In Israel the dead bodies of the worst criminals were sometimes hung on a tree (see, for instance, Josh. 8:29 and 10:26–27) as a sign that they were cursed by God (Deut. 21:23). To a pious Jew, as Paul says (Gal. 3:13), Jesus fell under just such a curse by hanging on a cross.

Until the third or fourth century, therefore, Christian art never portrayed Jesus on the cross and rarely even used the cross itself as a symbol. Yet the New Testament itself never dodges or downplays the hard reality of the cross. All four Gospels lead up to the crucifixion as a central dramatic climax. "When I came to you, brothers and sisters," Paul wrote to the Corinthians, "I did not come proclaiming the mystery of God to you in lofty words or wisdom. For I decided to know nothing among you except Jesus Christ, and him crucified" (1 Cor. 2:1–2).

To recover the original significance of Jesus' cross, we have to imagine ourselves back in the first century, in an impoverished Roman province torn apart by oppression, corruption, and the threat of religious rebellion. The Gospels provide an invaluable historical resource for such a project, but they need to be used with caution. The authors of the New Testament were simply not overly concerned about accuracy of detail. To take one example, in the first three Gospels the Last Supper takes place as a Passover meal. The Gospel of John moves everything back one day so that Jesus himself dies at the moment the Passover lamb would have been sacrificed. These writers are concerned to convey the meaning of the events they recount. They can treat chronology and other particulars quite casually.

It is important to be cautious about such matters, in part because the blood of Jesus is not the only blood that stains these stories. For centuries, anti-Jewish rabble-rousers quoted the Gospel narratives to show that "the Jews" were "Christ killers." Jews in Christian lands came to dread Holy Week as a time when they might face beatings or massacre.

Such interpretations misunderstand the original meaning of the New Testament. When the Gospels were written, Judaism was an officially recognized religion in the Roman Empire. Christians were struggling to survive, afraid of Roman persecution. Crucifixion was a *Roman* penalty (Jews executed by stoning), and therefore even the mention of the cross suggested to a Roman audience that the founder of this new religion must have been a political troublemaker. The more Christians blamed the Roman authorities for Jesus' death, the more they risked raising Roman suspicions and putting themselves in danger. No one at the time worried about giving license for Christian persecution of Jews—the tiny Christian community was in no position to persecute anybody.

Moreover, nearly all the authors of the New Testament were Jews born and raised. They took it for granted that Abraham's descendants were the chosen people of God; they knew that even their Gentile neighbors recognized the remarkable piety and faithfulness of the Jewish people. If one said that "Jews" had turned against Jesus, they understood that that meant *"even some* Jews," even some from among God's covenant people.

Of all the New Testament books, only the Fourth Gospel repeatedly identifies "the Jews" as the ones calling for Jesus' death. The great contemporary scholar Raymond Brown makes a persuasive case that "the Fourth Gospel uses the Jews as almost a technical title for the religious authorities, particularly those in Jerusalem, who are hostile to Jesus." He points out that in John 9:22, for instance, the parents of the blind man, clearly Jews themselves, are said to fear "the Jews"; in John 5:15 a former cripple, himself a Jew, informs "the Jews that it was Jesus who had made him well."[2] In this text, "the Jews" means the religious authorities of Jerusalem.

To begin this section by saying that Jesus was *condemned for blasphemy and sedition,* therefore, focuses on the relation of his death to the powers of his time, whether governmental or religious. Blasphemy represents a challenge to religious authority. Sedition means stirring up rebellion. Jesus was not a respectable citizen murdered by criminals. He suffered the death of a criminal at the hands of respectable citizens. The Roman Empire was not even a particularly wicked tyranny, but ruled more justly and tolerantly than most governments, and gave the Mediterranean world one of the longest stretches of peace in its history. Yet the Roman governor condemned this Jesus to the pain and shame of crucifixion. "The kings of the earth took their stand," Acts records Peter and John proclaiming in Jerusalem, ". . . and the rulers have gathered together/against the Lord and against his Messiah" (Acts 4:26). The historical role of the Jewish leaders in Jerusalem is less clear, but some of them may well have felt this new leader, with his ragtag following and his threats to the Temple, enough of a threat to the established order to justify encouraging the Romans to put him to death. There is at any rate no evidence that they protested. And these were the established religious leaders of God's covenant people.

The Gospels help us understand. Jesus had consistently angered people in authority. He spent time with prostitutes and tavern owners, riffraff despised by pious people, and with tax collectors, who were known to be corrupt and all too cooperative with the hated Roman occupiers. He challenged traditional customs; he forgave sins on his own authority. When he encountered local businessmen providing pilgrims at the Temple in Jerusalem with animals to be sacrificed and Temple coinage, he overturned their stalls and drove them out of the Temple.

Jesus was no Zealot; he did not try to organize a military rebellion against Rome. But in first-century Palestine there was no such thing as a "purely religious" question. Many who hoped for a Messiah expected a revolutionary leader who would drive out the Romans. The very term Messiah or its Greek translation "Christ" meant "anointed one," anointed by God like the ancient kings of Israel. That implied a claim to authority higher than that of Roman law.

More generally, the Roman Empire claimed that its legions constituted the world's best hope for peace, that imperial glory was among the highest of human accomplishments, and that no power was greater than that of the divine emperor. To take Jesus seriously was to challenge all those assumptions. If Pontius Pilate saw in Jesus a threat to imperial claims, he was, finally, not mistaken.

The Jesus *unjustly condemned for blasphemy and sedition* was in short an outsider who lived in solidarity with the poor and the despised, at odds with respectable religious authorities, and was executed by the state as a potential rebel.

> He was despised and rejected by others;
>   a man of suffering and acquainted with infirmity;
> and as one from whom others hide their faces
>   he was despised, and we held him of no account.
>
> (Isa. 53:3)

We Presbyterians have often drawn our numbers from among the respectable folk of society. Sometimes we get nervous about welcoming into the church those our society deems unrespectable, whether they be the poor, the politically controversial, victims of AIDS, or whatever. We need to remember that it is in an unrespectable Jesus that we put our trust, and to think about what that means for our lives.

This *Jesus was crucified*. It seems odd to state the event so central to our faith with a passive verb. And yet the oddity turns out to be appropriate, for the story of Jesus' way to death combines the active and the passive in a complex and important way.

Jesus was not a suicide. His suffering and dying was something done to him. He faced death with dread, fear, weeping. He prayed that, "if it were possible, the hour might pass from him" (Mark 14:35). He did not want to die. In the mounting drama of the story of his last days, he gradually lost human choice. He could easily enough have stayed away from Jerusalem. Once there, escape would have been more difficult, but even in the Garden of Gethsemane he still stood a chance of slipping off into the night. Even after his arrest, he could have begged for mercy or tried to assure Pilate that it was all a mistake. But on the cross, his hands and feet nailed to the wood, he lost all human freedom.

Yet the story keeps reminding us that this broken body is the Lord. He stands before Pilate, oddly in control of the situation. John's Gospel has him tell his disciples, "I lay down my life in order to take it up again. No one takes it from me, but I lay it down of my own accord. I have power to lay it down, and I have power to take it up again" (John 10:17–18). Even hanging on the cross, Jesus forgives a fellow victim and promises, "Today you will be with me in Paradise" (Luke 23:43). In the end, Luke says, he cried out in a loud voice, "Father, into your hands I commend my spirit," and breathed his last—as if dying itself were his free choice (Luke 23:46; see also John 19:30).

This odd juxtaposition of passive and active, powerlessness and power, points to a category central to Reformed interpretations of Christ's work—*obedience*. "Christ abolished sin, banished the separation between us and God, and acquired righteousness to render God favorable and kindly toward us," Calvin wrote, "by the whole course of his *obedience*" (*Institutes* 2.16.5). Christ secured our justification, the Westminster Confession says, "by his *obedience* and death" (6.070). (Emphasis added, both instances.)

To obey is to submit and yet to submit freely. The story would be altogether different if Jesus had *wanted* to die. It would also be completely different if he had been dragged kicking and screaming to his death. In obedience, he freely accepted a fate he did not seek. Yet in his acceptance of God's will for his life, he is at one with that will. In the end he has done exactly what he set out to do, and he seems, remarkably enough, the freest person we can imagine. His obedience to death seems a triumph.

In the story as we read it, Jesus becomes one with God in his obedience, and the way he achieves his triumph therefore tells us something about the power of this strange God who loves in ways we can hardly imagine. We assume that one achieves power by growing stronger, asserting oneself, seizing the initiative. Build up your military defenses! Fight the corporate battle! Learn to be assertive! These are the lessons of our society. On his way to death, however, Jesus grows weaker, gives up the initiative.

> He humbled himself
>   and became obedient to the point of death—
>   even death on a cross.
>
> (Phil. 2:8)

Yet from the perspective of God, this proves the path to a kind of victory. That should make us stop and think—think about the power of love, and how God's love can work through what looks at first, to human eyes, like powerlessness.

Jesus died, *suffering the depths of human pain*. It was not what we usually picture as a heroic death. The contemporary German theologian Jürgen Moltmann makes the point vividly:

> Socrates died a wise man. Cheerfully and calmly he drank the cup of hemlock. . . . The Zealot martyrs who were crucified after the unsuccessful revolt against the Romans died conscious of their righteousness in the sight of God and looked forward

to their resurrection to eternal life. . . . The wise men of the
Stoics demonstrated to the tyrants in the arena, where they
were torn to pieces by wild animals, their inner liberty and their
superiority. . . . Jesus clearly died in a different way. His death
was not a "fine death." The synoptic gospels agree that he was
"greatly distressed and troubled" (Mark 14:33) and that his
soul was sorrowful even to death. He died "with loud cries and
tears," according to the Epistle to the Hebrews (Hebrews 5:7)
According to Mark 15:37 he died with a loud, incoherent cry.[3]

The physical pain of crucifixion was excruciating, but it was
in some ways the least of Christ's suffering. If we imagine that
Jesus had only to endure a few hours of physical pain, secure in
the comfort of God's presence and confident in the hope of
resurrection, then we have not understood his agony. He
sweated blood, the Gospels tell us (Luke 22:44); he cried out,
"My God, my God, why have you forsaken me?" (Mark
15:34)—the only time he did not call to God as "Father." "No
more terrible abyss can be conceived," Calvin wrote, "than to
feel yourself forsaken and estranged from God; and when you
call upon him, not to be heard" *(Institutes* 2.16.11). "To say
that he was pretending . . . is a foul evasion. We must with assurance, therefore, confess Christ's sorrow . . . unless we are
ashamed of the cross" (*Institutes* 2.16.12).

The Apostles' Creed declares that Christ "descended into
hell." Christians of many different traditions unite in saying
that line of the creed, but they have not agreed on what it
means. In the thirteenth century, Thomas Aquinas organized
the tentative remarks of earlier theologians into what became
the standard Catholic interpretation: After death, Christ went
to hell to rescue the great figures of the Old Testament and
carry them up into heaven (*Summa Theologiae* 3.52.2, 4–6, 8).
Christ's "harrowing of hell" became a favorite subject for poets
and artists alike. For Luther too the "descent into hell" meant
that Christ had gone to hell after his death—though for Luther
the central point of the trip was the defeat of the devil rather
than the rescue of the heroes and heroines of ancient Israel.

Calvin, however, in a view anticipated by Nicholas of Cusa
and a few others in the Middle Ages, said that it was in the

agony of doubt and fear Christ underwent *before* death that he "descended into hell." "Hell" was the agony of facing death without the presence of God. It was not enough for Christ to die; "he must also grapple hand to hand with the armies of hell and the dread of everlasting death . . . suffering in his soul the terrible torments of a condemned and forsaken man" (*Institutes* 2.16.10).

When we say that Christ was "fully human," when we say that "though he was in the form of God, . . ./[he] emptied himself,/taking the form of a slave" (Phil. 2:6–7), this is where we are finally led. Christ was not an undisturbed God living in a human body, but "*fully* human"—subject to doubts and fears and the agony of sensing that God had abandoned him.

Therefore those who suffer the worst of human agonies can know that Christ understands. "For we do not have a high priest who is unable to sympathize with our weaknesses, but we have one who in every respect has been tested as we are" (Heb. 4:15). Having doubts and being afraid are not sinful; they're part of the natural condition of being human, and nothing to be ashamed of. They go right along with tackling a tough job. Jesus shows us that.

But Jesus' suffering also assures us that we do not go through hell alone, whatever our particular hell may be. When the Heidelberg Catechism works through explaining the Apostles' Creed, it discusses the "comfort" we can find in each particular phrase. With respect to "descended into hell," it says my comfort is "that in my severest tribulations I may be assured that Christ my Lord had redeemed me from hellish anxieties and torment by the unspeakable anguish, pains, and terrors which he suffered in his soul both on the cross and before" (4.044). Somone who loves us found the way through the darkness back to the light. Because Christ went down that road, through the valley of the shadow of death, none of us ever again needs to feel that we travel it alone.

"The central Christian belief," C. S. Lewis wrote, "is that Christ's death has somehow put us right with God and given us a fresh start. Theories as to how it did this are another matter. A good many different theories have been held as to how it

works; what all Christians are agreed on is that it does work."[4]
That's good Reformed theology, for the Reformed tradition
has agreed that on the cross Jesus was *giving his life for the sins
of the world* but has never chosen a single "orthodox" way to
explain the significance of his suffering and death. As the
Confession of 1967 says,

> God's reconciling act in Jesus Christ is a mystery which the
> Scriptures describe in various ways. It is called the sacrifice of a
> lamb, a shepherd's life given for his sheep, atonement by a
> priest; again it is ransom of a slave, payment of debt, vicarious
> satisfaction of a legal penalty, and victory over the powers of
> evil. These are expressions of a truth which remains beyond the
> reach of all theory in the depths of God's love. (9.09)

That recognition of the diversity in the ways Christians can
think about what Christ did for us was nothing new in 1967.
Calvin himself mentioned a series of possibilities: "If the death
of Christ be our redemption, then we were captives; if it be satisfaction, we were debtors; if it be atonement, we were guilty;
if it be cleansing, we were unclean."[5] One can find those images and others besides in Reformed confessions. They propose
different ways we can think about the meaning of Christ's suffering, death, and resurrection:

—If you were a slave, someone else could pay your "redemption" and secure your freedom. We are enslaved to sin, and
   Christ redeems us.

—If you owed a debt beyond your capacity to pay it, someone else could pay it for you. Our sins against God put us
   in God's debt in a way that we can never repay. Christ pays
   the debt on our behalf.

—If you were held hostage by evil forces, and unable to escape, you needed someone who could defeat your captors
   and free you. We are entrapped by the powers of evil, and
   Christ takes them on and defeats them.

—If your relationship with God had been damaged, you
   could restore it by offering a proper sacrifice, by giving to
   God something pure and of value. Christ sacrifices himself

on our behalf, and thereby brings us back into fellowship with God. (The word "atonement" derives from "at-one-ment"—making us again at one with God.)

All such accounts are, as the Confession of 1967 said, "expressions of a truth which remains beyond the reach of all theory in the depths of God's love." But we can note some features of that truth. A story encountered in the work of several authors warns against one sort of misunderstanding: a small child, given an account of how Christ died for our sins to redeem us before God, cries out, "I love Jesus. But I hate God." Sometimes we do tell the story in a way that makes it sound as if the love of Christ overcame an unforgiving and angry God.

But that gets the story all wrong. "*God* so loved the world that he gave his only Son" (John 3:16, emphasis added). Dying on a cross is agony, but so is watching the sufferings of a beloved child. "In this is love, not that we loved God but that he loved us and sent his Son to be the atoning sacrifice for our sins" (1 John 4:10). Whatever happened at the cross, it was an action that also showed the love of the one Jesus called "Father." It is finally the work of the triune God that reconciles us. (See the discussion of line 54 in chapter 10 for the role of the Holy Spirit.) As Calvin put it, "God did not begin to love us when we were reconciled to him by the blood of his Son, but he loved us before the creation of the world" (*Institutes* 2.16.4).

On the other hand, it is not simply that Christ's suffering and death help *us* to realize the love God had for us all along. "As God hates sin, we are also hated by him as far as we are sinners."[6] It is not just that we misunderstand; there is something objectively wrong in how we stand with God, something that needs to be put right. God never stops loving us, but when we sin that love, as love can do, can take the form of real anger. As Calvin put it, God "both hated and loved us at the same time. He hated us being different from what he had made us; but as our iniquity had not destroyed entirely his work in us, he could at the same time in every one of us hate what we had done and love what he had made" (*Institutes* 2.16.4).

As one more model for how Christ puts things right, consider the betrayal of a friendship and how that betrayal can be healed. If I betray a friend, then the bond of our friendship is

damaged. My friend will be hurt and angry. In human friend-
ships, no doubt, selfishness and pettiness always play some part
in such reactions, but even perfect love would still feel hurt and
anger at betrayal. If betrayal from one side of the relationship
does not cause any pain on the other side, then there was not
much love there in the first place.

Sometimes, if I have done wrong to a friend, I can make it
right. But sometimes the wrong is irremediable. Nothing I can
do could fully fix what I have broken. Suppose my friend still
loves me. What could such a friend do? To say, "Don't worry, it
doesn't matter," is to deny the seriousness of our love. If it *really*
does not matter, then we were scarcely friends. To say that the
wound is deep and cannot be healed would be more loving than
that. But a loving friend might say, "I am wounded. I am angry.
That is the proof that I cared about you. It costs me to reach out
toward you, to try to trust you again. Yet I love you still, and so
I will take on that pain and bear that cost, because I do not want
us driven apart forever by the consequences of what you did."
That seems to be how it is with love and betrayal—just as a slave
cannot be freed without paying a redemption, just as prisoners
cannot be freed without taking on their captors, just as someone
has to pay off a debt, so love betrayed cannot be healed without
cost. It hardly seems fair that the one who has been in the right
should pay the cost of the wrong, but love does not worry too
much about fairness.

All of us have betrayed God's love. "We rebel against God;
we hide from our Creator. . . . [We] exploit neighbor and nature, and threaten death to the planet entrusted to our care.
We deserve God's condemnation" (lines 33–39). God does
not say that the wound is easily healed, for that would deny the
depth of God's love.

> Rather, your iniquities have been barriers
>   between you and your God,
> and your sins have hidden his face from you
>   so that he does not hear.
>
> (Isa. 59:2)

Calvin put it this way: "No one can descend into himself
and seriously consider what he is without feeling God's wrath

and hostility toward him. Accordingly he must anxiously seek ways and means to appease God—and this demands a satisfaction" (*Institutes* 2.16.1).

But God does not leave us to our sins. "Since all have sinned and fall short of the glory of God; they are now justified by his grace as a gift, through the redemption that is in Christ Jesus, whom God put forward as a sacrifice of atonement" (Rom. 3:23–25). This is what Christians have meant by "vicarious atonement"—that the price of bringing us back to be at one with God is borne vicariously, not by us but by Jesus Christ. "In Christ God was reconciling the world to himself" (2 Cor. 5:19). Love betrayed can never be reconciled without cost, and in the cross we see the cost God was willing to pay. It is, first to last, a story about God's love, but it is a story about how healing love sometimes involves suffering. Our sin matters; God cares that we have turned away. But we remain God's people, and God does not turn away from us. The Scots Confession captures part of the essence of the story in a complex net of imagery:

> So we confess . . . that our Lord Jesus offered himself a voluntary sacrifice unto his Father for us, that he suffered contradiction for sinners, that he was wounded and plagued for our transgressions, that he, the clean innocent lamb of God, was condemned in the presence of an earthly judge, that we should be absolved before the judgment seat of our God; that he suffered not only the cruel death of the cross, which was accursed by the sentence of God; but also that he suffered for a season the wrath of his Father which sinners had deserved. But yet we avow that he remained the only, well beloved, and blessed Son of his Father even in the midst of his anguish and torment which he suffered in body and soul to make full atonement for the sins of his people. (3.09)

5. Resurrection
(Lines 23–26)

23   God raised this Jesus from the dead,
24   vindicating his sinless life,
25   breaking the power of sin and evil,
26   delivering us from death to life eternal.

"Christ is risen! Christ is risen indeed!" This is the good news of Easter; it is the good news of Christian faith. The meaning we give to Jesus' suffering and death comes only in the light of the resurrection. Jesus' first disciples were afraid and despairing after the crucifixion, and they were not wrong. If the cross had been the end of the story, then it would be the story of one more good person who failed. But shortly after Jesus' death something else happened.

The New Testament never describes the event of the resurrection itself. What it does tell us is that shortly after Jesus' death some of his followers encountered him and discovered that the friend and teacher they had thought dead and a failure still lived. Their experiences reached beyond the limits of human imagination and human language. They spoke of them like people stammering and stuttering in the face of the simply indescribable. Paul's companions on the road to Damascus, the book of Acts reports, heard a voice from heaven but saw no one (Acts 9:7). Or, alternatively, they saw a light but did not hear a voice (Acts 22:9). The Gospels mention an empty tomb, but Paul does not refer to it. In John's Gospel, Jesus tells Mary not to "hold on to" (or, as some translations have it, "touch") him (John 20:17) but later invites Thomas to reach out his hand and put it in his side (John 20:27). He mysteriously appears and disappears; he eats fish (Luke 24:43). Attempts to sort out a chronological sequence of these appearances or to get a clear account of what it was like to encounter the risen Jesus break down in the face of shifting analogies and frustrating silences. These texts have a different sort of message to tell us.

God did something—that's the place to start. *God raised this Jesus from the dead.* It was not simply that, after Jesus' death, people began to realize some truth about him they could have known all along. Jesus died feeling abandoned by God, humiliated and accursed. We do not take the horror of the cross seriously if we think that it was already a triumph. If God did not act to raise this Jesus from the dead, then, as Paul says, "our proclamation has been in vain and your faith has been in vain. We are even found to be misrepresenting God, because we testified of God that he raised Christ" (1 Cor. 15:14–15). Jesus was really dead, and then the God who can make things out of nothing made life out of death, and only in response to that act did Christian faith become possible.

The story of Jesus' death and resurrection is, therefore, not a story about how death has no real power; it is a story about how God overcame even the power of death. The point is not that human beings are somehow by nature immortal or that we are being silly when we are afraid of death. Jesus Christ, who was fully human, really died, and death is frightening, terrible. It is only because of the power of a loving God that we have hope that reaches beyond death.

God raised *this Jesus from the dead*—what happened was a "resurrection," a term with a special meaning in the context of ancient Jewish thought. By the time of Jesus some Jews (but not all—see Acts 23:8, where Paul gets himself out of a tight spot by setting some of his Jewish accusers against others on just this issue) expected that at the end of the present evil age God would raise the righteous dead to a triumphant new life. Resurrection was the sign of the beginning of a new age, in which the world would be transformed:

> Your dead shall live, their corpses shall rise.
> O dwellers in the dust, awake and sing for joy!
> (Isa. 26:19)

So, if Jesus has been resurrected, then all the rules of the way things are are up for grabs. A new age with altogether new rules has begun. Jesus was not simply restored to life, like Lazarus or the son of the widow of Nain. They were brought back to the same old life, and would in due time die again. But Christ, "being raised from the dead, will never die again; death no longer has dominion over him" (Rom. 6:9).

In the context of Jewish resurrection hopes, what was most surprising was that something which was expected for *many people* at the *end* of history should happen to *one person* in the *middle* of history. Jesus is the "first fruits" of the hoped-for resurrection, the early Christians said (1 Cor. 15:23), come "into an inheritance that is imperishable, undefiled, and unfading" (1 Peter 1:4).

But what was it like to be resurrected, or even to encounter the resurrected Jesus? Paul does not give us much help:

> But someone will ask, "How are the dead raised? With what kind of body do they come?" Fool! What you sow does not come to life unless it dies. And as for what you sow, you do not sow the body that is to be, but a bare seed, perhaps of wheat or of some other grain. But God gives it a body as he has chosen, and to each kind of seed its own body. . . . There are both heavenly bodies and earthly bodies, but the glory of the heavenly is one thing, and that of the earthly is another. . . . So it is with the resurrection of the dead. What is sown is perishable, what is raised is imperishable. It is sown in dishonor, it is raised in glory. It is sown in weakness, it is raised in power. It is sown a physical body, it is raised a spiritual body. (1 Cor. 15:35–38, 40, 42–44)

Paul talks confusingly of "heavenly bodies" and "spiritual bodies," with as little in common with our earthly bodies as a plant has with its seed. Still, some reference to a body does seem part of what "resurrection" means. Jewish and Christian faith, unlike much of Greek philosophy, does not teach that the goal of human life is to free our souls from our evil bodies. "Look at my hands and my feet," Luke reports the risen Christ saying; "see that it is I myself. Touch me and see; for a ghost does not have flesh and bones as you see that I have" (Luke 24:39). Being embodied is part of what makes me "I myself"; having a body is part of what it is to be human. It is part of the good way that God made us. (See line 29.) Our bodies are temples of the Holy Spirit within us (1 Cor. 6:19). Therefore, Calvin says, "it would be utterly absurd that the bodies which God has dedicated to himself as temples should fall away into filth without hope of resurrection. What of the fact that they are also members of Christ? Or that God commands all their parts to be sanctified to him?" (*Institutes* 3.25.7).

If our bodies are part of who we are, then hope for our life beyond death must somehow include the hope that our bodiliness is not lost. If the resurrected Jesus was the firstfruits of the hope that awaits us all, then the Jesus his disciples encountered must have been somehow embodied. Those "somehows" imply a good bit of caution, but it is not a caution invented by modern skepticism. The New Testament texts themselves warn us against too much speculation about this different form of embodiedness.

They give us accounts from witnesses, accounts of how encounters with the Jesus who was alive after all changed their lives forever. The first of those witnesses were women. In that time and place, women were generally not even allowed to testify in court—their testimony was thought too unreliable. When Paul assembled the closest thing we have to a summary of the eyewitness evidence, he very nearly leaves the women out altogether (1 Cor. 15:5–7; he mentions women only among the five hundred brothers and sisters). Yet in the face of all the political, cultural reasons not to do it, every one of the Gospels begins the resurrection story with the witness of women. Just as the Hebrew rebellion against slavery in Egypt began with the midwives who "feared God" and "did not do as the king of Egypt commanded them," (Ex. 1:17), just as the story of the incarnation begins with a woman, Mary, and her encounter with an angel, so the story of the resurrection begins on the first day of the week, early in the morning, when women who had loved Jesus went to his tomb and then returned with news strange and terrifying, but wonderful beyond imagining.

The resurrection made a difference. It made a difference, first of all, in what one could say about Jesus. *God raised this Jesus from the dead, vindicating his sinless life.* The book of Acts reports that the first Christian sermons consistently emphasized, having told something of Jesus' life, that it was *this Jesus* that God had raised from the dead: "This Jesus God raised up" (Acts 2:32). "This Jesus is 'the stone that was rejected by you, the builders/it has become the cornerstone' " (Acts 4:11). The good news is not merely that someone has been raised from the dead, but that *Jesus* has been raised from the dead ("the same Jesus Christ our Lord," Second Helvetic Confession 5.073). If the Emperor Nero had been raised from the dead, or even Socrates the virtuous philosopher, that would have been very different news. The Jesus who taught about love and promised hope, who spent time with prostitutes and other sinners, who got in trouble with political authorities, who healed the sick, bound up the brokenhearted, and called all to repent and believe the gospel—God raised *this* Jesus from the dead. Jesus' claim to authority, his claim to a unique relationship with God, was not blasphemy after all. His story did not end with his death as an accursed outcast. A life that had seemed a failure turned out to give us the clue for what human life is meant to be. An apparent blasphemer gives us the model for knowing about God.

In raising Jesus from the dead, God was also *breaking the power of sin and evil.* From the New Testament itself to the words of Easter hymns, the news of the resurrection comes as news of a victory: "Death has been swallowed up in victory" (1 Cor. 15:54).

> The strife is o'er, the battle done,
> The victory of life is won;
> The song of triumph has begun.
> Alleluia.[1]

The very idea of a victory implies enemies to be defeated, and the enemies defeated at Christ's resurrection seem to be the powers of sin and death.

In Hebrew culture, the idea of resurrection had developed less in the context of questions about life after death than out of concerns about justice. The people of ancient Israel were in general willing to accept the idea that if you had a rich and full life and many descendants, that would be good enough, and when you died you were dead. But there are those good people who suffer throughout their lives and die young, forgotten, without heirs:

> They have perished as though they had never existed;
>> they have become as though they had never been born.
>>> (Ecclus. 44:9)

What about them?

If such people are to share in God's promises, Jews began to think in the few centuries before the time of Jesus, then they must somehow be restored to life. There must be hope of resurrection.

> O Lord, in distress they sought you.
> . . . .
>
> We gave birth only to wind.
> We have won no victories on earth.

But God will prove faithful even to those who seem abandoned:

> Your dead shall live, their corpses shall rise.
> O dwellers in the dust, awake and sing for joy!
>> (Isa. 26:16, 18–19)

The hope of resurrection was not simply that there is life beyond death, but that God is just and merciful, and the forces that seem to overwhelm people, whatever those forces may be, will not finally triumph.

For the Bible, after all, "death" does not mean merely the end of physical life. When Paul cries out, "Wretched man that I am! Who will rescue me from this body of death?" (Rom. 7:24), he does not mean simply that he is going to die someday. He means that even now, as he lives from day to day, the powers of death have gotten control over his life.

The same thing can happen to us. Sometimes we try to make ourselves rather than God the center of our lives. Sometimes we try to put our families or companies or countries or causes, rather than God, at the center of our lives. Either way, the thought that we might cease to be, or that other human beings or human institutions might cease to be, leaves a gaping hole at the center of everything. We are terrified of death. That fear of death leads us to try all the harder to grasp the wealth or power or fame that could give us a sense that we control our lives after all. It does not work, and human struggles for wealth and power have a way of bringing yet more death into the world. "Death came through sin, and so death spread to all because all have sinned," Paul says (Rom. 5:12). Whatever else that may mean, it seems a simple statement of fact about our experience. It is as if there really are powers called Sin and Death powerfully at work in our world.

But Christ's resurrection can change all that. Jesus did not cling to life, but gave it up for others. He did not seek power and wealth, but taught love and sought to serve. Yet he was the one to triumph over death. Maybe we have been going about things the wrong way. Maybe if we give up our doomed efforts to prove that we are too good to be destroyed, God will give us the news that we are safe simply because God loves us. If we do not have to try to prove ourselves, if we do not have to fight for survival, then those forces of Sin and Death have been defeated. Christ has defeated them and "brought life again to us who were subject to death and its bondage" (Scots Confession 3.10).

That means we can start living differently. We can stop being afraid. We do not have to keep trying to amass enough from this world to achieve security—an endeavor doomed to failure and leading to ever greater selfishness. We do not have to play according to the rules of the forces of death. In the words of a recent statement of faith by Korean Presbyterians:

> The resurrection of Jesus means that death, the ultimate foe of man, is conquered by life and by the victory of justice and love. It is a power which opens God's future and sheds light on the world. It strengthens the weak, raises up the lowly, restores the rights of those who are unlawfully treated, brings about the victory of the righteous who have been defeated, and grants life to the dead.[2]

In raising Jesus from the dead, God was *delivering us from death to life eternal.* If Christ's resurrection "break[s] the power of sin and evil," that makes a difference for our lives here and now—it is not merely a hope about some future beyond death. But that difference for here and now is not in itself enough. Our world, here and now, does not look as if the forces of sin and death have been defeated. Karl Barth used the image of a great battle: even when the battle has already been won, isolated troops, unaware of the news, continue to fight, and their fighting can be savage and bloody. So we still live in a world where the battle rages on, even though it has already been won. A Declaration of Faith, a confessional statement written for the Presbyterian Church in the U.S. in the 1970s, speaks of Christ's Lordship, which is hidden but real:

> We declare that Jesus is Lord.
> His resurrection is a decisive victory
> over the powers that deform and destroy human life.
> His lordship is hidden.
> The world appears to be dominated by people and systems
> that do not acknowledge his rule.
> But his lordship is real.
> It demands our loyalty and sets us free
> from the fear of all lesser lords who threaten us.[3]

It is because we believe Christ's Lordship will not always be hidden that we believe it is real. We can live confidently in a world full of tragedy and ambiguity, in other words, because we have hope. Our faith is not *just* about the future—it makes a difference here and now. But we see things here and now differently in part because we see them in the light of hope we have for the future.

The New Testament keeps that tension between present and future in its discussions of eternal life. It is a gift already received by those who have faith: "Anyone who hears my word and believes him who sent me has eternal life, and does not come under judgment, but has passed from death to life" (John 5:24; see also John 3:36 and 10:27–28). But it is also a hope for the future: "Truly I tell you, there is no one who has left house or brothers or sisters or mother or father or children or fields, for my sake and for the sake of the good news, who will not receive a hundredfold now in this age—houses, brothers and sisters, mothers and children, and fields with persecutions—and in the age to come eternal life" (Mark 10:29–30).

This "eternal life" is not just life that lasts a very long time, even forever, but a different kind of life. There's an old story about a man granted any wish who asked to live forever, and then lived out an eternal misery of senility and decay because he forgot to ask for eternal youth. But even being young forever might still leave one subject to temptation, uncertainty, and fear—still under the power of death.

When we say that God is eternal, we do not merely mean that God lives forever, but mean that God is not subject to the vicissitudes and uncertainties of changing time.

> Long ago you laid the foundation of the earth,
>   and the heavens are the work of your hands.
> They will perish, but you endure;
>   they will all wear out like a garment.
> You change them like clothing, and they pass away;
>   but you are the same, and your years have no end.
>   (Ps. 102:25–27)

There is no worrisome uncertainty in the future of God, no turning point at which what was formerly unsettled becomes secure or the formerly secure comes into doubt. In that sense, "with the Lord one day is like a thousand years, and a thousand years are like one day" (2 Peter 3:8).

"Everything seems to us confused and mixed up," Calvin once wrote, "but all the while a constant quiet and serenity ever remain in heaven" (*Institutes* 1.17.1). It is to such eternal life that Christ's resurrection delivers us from the powers of death. The present always remains ambiguous. Shafts of sunlight appear, but shadows return. Even the most devout Christians remain daring but afraid, unexpectedly free but still entrapped, encountering glimpses of eternal life but still living amid death. "The resurrection of Jesus is God's sign that he will consummate his work of creation and reconciliation beyond death and bring fulfillment to the new life begun in Christ" (Confession of 1967, 9.26).

Trust in God,
Whom Jesus Called Abba, Father

6. God—Abba—Father
(Lines 27–28)

27 We trust in God,
28   whom Jesus called Abba, Father.

A reminder about the structure of this statement: These lines begin a new section, about the first Person of the Trinity. Having begun with Christ, we can now identify that first Person directly: the One *Jesus called Abba, Father,* the One who raised Jesus from the dead.

The name appropriate to this Person raises a good bit of controversy in contemporary theology. Theologians such as Sallie McFague and Paul Tillich remind us that the symbols we use about God help us understand God, but they also affect the way we understand the things we use for symbols.[1] When people who lived under a monarchy referred to God as "King," for instance, that helped shape the way they thought about God, but it also gave their kings a kind of secondhand divinity. Similarly, to speak of God always as "Father," one traditional name for this Person, risks leading us to think that the father ought to be a kind of god within the family. Since that no longer fits the way most of us think about families, we look for different ways to speak about God that still remain faithful to the Christian tradition. We at least understand Celie's complaint in Alice Walker's novel *The Color Purple:* "When I found out I thought God was white, and a man, I lost interest."[2] We want to be sure to provide a different understanding of God.

This Statement of Faith begins with the triune formula of Paul's apostolic benediction: "The grace of our Lord Jesus Christ, the love of God, and the communion of the Holy Spirit" (lines 2–4; 2 Cor. 13:13). That biblical language refers to the first Person of the Trinity simply as "God." One could argue that that is confusing; all three Persons are "God," and perhaps the word used without qualification ought to be applied only to the one triune God—the whole Trinity. Yet this reference to the first Person as "God" has always been common in the Christian tradition. The Scots Confession, for instance, says, "When the fullness of time came, God sent his Son, his eternal wisdom, the substance of his glory, into the world" (3.06).[3] Even the Nicene Creed begins, "We believe in one God the Father Almighty, . . . and in one Lord Jesus Christ, the only-begotten Son of God," distinguishing the "Son of God" from "God."

Line 27 is therefore quite traditional in beginning this section by saying, "We trust in God." But we still need some specification of this particular Person: What sets this section apart? In prayers and creeds, the most common identification has been to speak of "the Father," but the Christian tradition has also generally wanted to emphasize that God is in important ways *unlike* human fathers. In Karl Barth's words, "Our natural human father is not our Creator. He is not the lord of our existence, not for a moment the lord of our life, far less of our death. In calling God our Father, Scripture adopts an analogy, only to break through it at once."[4]

The language of "God the Father" is common in our tradition, and in some ways appropriate enough—God loves us and watches over us and encourages us to grow in the ways that a good father does. But it is language subject to dire misuse and many misunderstandings. Christians have long wanted to warn against those misunderstandings, and contemporary theologians have made us particularly conscious of their dangers. What we need, then, is some way to acknowledge that traditional language but also to undercut it a little, warning ourselves to be careful how we use it.

The best resource for such subversion seems to come from Jesus himself. Three times the New Testament uses the word

"Abba" (Mark 14:36; Rom. 8:15; Gal. 4:6); these are among the very few times the Greek text quotes in Aramaic, the language Jesus himself usually spoke. Moreover, all three passages come at crucial points in the text. Mark is describing Jesus' prayer in the Garden of Gethsemane, just before he sets off on the last journey to the cross: "Abba, Father, for you all things are possible; remove this cup from me; yet, not what I want, but what you want" (Mark 14:36). Paul is in both the other passages reaching a climax in his account of life in oneness with Christ as children of God:

> And because you are children, God has sent the Spirit of his Son into our hearts, crying, "Abba! Father!" So you are no longer a slave but a child, and if a child then also an heir, through God.
>
> (Gal. 4:6–7)[5]

A good many recent scholars hold that this use of "Abba" was not only characteristic of Jesus himself but an important innovation.[6] "Abba" was a familiar, family word, like "Daddy" in English, that would have struck many of Jesus' contemporaries as shocking in its informality. Scholars continue to debate some of these historical issues, but it does at least seem clear that when Jesus prayed to his "Abba," he was implying an unparalleled intimacy with God. Paul is making a daring claim when he calls on his readers to think of themselves as co-heirs in Christ, who in the Spirit can also call, "Abba! Father!"

In his own day, then, Jesus seems to have challenged some traditional language about God. We are faithful to him if we think of appropriate ways of raising similar challenges in our time. In particular, the word "Abba" would in Jesus' day not have been an affirmation of traditional patriarchy, but a challenge to it. That word "Abba" is strange to us—literally foreign, just as it was to the original Greek readers of the New Testament. Perhaps its very foreignness can remind us to mistrust our usual assumptions and stay prepared for surprises when we trust in the God Jesus called "Abba, Father."

7. Creation
(Lines 29–32)

29   In sovereign love God created the world good
30   and makes everyone equally in God's image,
31   male and female, of every race and people,
32   to live as one community.

> In the beginning when God created the heavens and the earth,
> the earth was a formless void and darkness covered the face of
> the deep, while a wind from God swept over the face of the wa-
> ters. Then God said, "Let there be light"; and there was light.
>
>   (Gen. 1:1–3)

The opening passages of the book of Genesis occasion much
debate and much misunderstanding. We live in a culture where
too many people believe that science is truth and poetry is "just
poetry." So they conclude that the first chapters of Genesis are
either accurate science or just false, and there are votes for both
sides. But a great poem can convey more truth—about love, or
pain, or how things are, or what it means to be human—than a
dozen scientific treatises. The first chapters of Genesis are not a
poem, exactly; they represent a literary form more alien to
most of us, a kind of saga of the origins of things. They convey
truth in roughly the way that a poem does. They are not accurate science; they are not meant to be. Still, they are true; they
have important things to teach us about God and ourselves
and the universe around us. If we try to make them into science, then scientists have a right to object. On the other hand,

if scientists claim that their empirical inquiries can answer ultimate questions about the purpose of the universe, then we in turn have a right to claim that they are overstepping their proper realm of expertise.

The God described in Genesis created *in sovereign love*. We tend to think of sovereignty and love almost as opposites. Sovereignty means power, and we are inclined to fear that love means weakness. Our Reformed confessions, however, tend to mention God's sovereignty and love together. Divine love is not a sign of weakness; divine power is not brutal intimidation. God is most fully loving in ruling all creation for good, and most sovereign in loving. A carpenter's son on a cross, dying in love, after all, turns out to be more powerful than all the legions of any empire. "For God's foolishness is wiser than human wisdom, and God's weakness is stronger than human strength" (1 Cor. 1:25).

Creation, this phrase of the statement reminds us, is already an act of God's love. In the creation stories of many other cultures, the creating deity has to subdue evil forces that threaten the divine will, or creates for the sake of some benefit the gods will derive from creation. In Genesis, God does not *have* to create, nor does God create as some act of self-protection or self-interest, but rather creates out of pure goodness, pure love. In C. S. Lewis's phrase, God "loves into existence purely superfluous creatures."[1]

That creation is an act of the triune God. We can occasionally refer to the first Person of the Trinity, the One Jesus called Abba, Father as "the Creator," but the reference is not technically correct if it implies that Word and Spirit play no part in creation.

In Genesis 1 (as in John 1), God creates by *speaking*—the Word of God is the agent of creation.

> By the word of the Lord the heavens were made,
>   and all their host by the breath of his mouth.
>
> (Ps. 33:6)

Part of the point of this particular image is the *effortlessness* of divine creation; in contrast to the creators in stories of other cultures, this God does not strive and struggle but simply speaks and it is done. Christians also believe, however, that the Word that creates is the Word that became incarnate in Jesus Christ. "He is the image of the invisible God, the firstborn of all creation; for in him all things in heaven and on earth were created. . . . He himself is before all things, and in him all things hold together" (Col. 1:15–17).

The Holy Spirit also has a part to play in the act of creation.

> O Lord, how manifold are your works!
> In wisdom you have made them all;
> the earth is full of your creatures. . . .
> When you send forth your spirit, they are created.
> (Ps. 104:24, 30)

At the beginning of the story of Creation, when "the earth was a formless void and darkness covered the face of the deep, . . . a wind from God swept over the face of the waters" (Gen. 1:2). That wind (the Hebrew word *ruach* can be translated as "wind" or "breath" or "spirit") is the breath or Spirit of God.

So what? What does it matter that all three Persons of the Trinity are at work in creation? For one thing, if we start assigning different tasks to different Persons of the Trinity, then we are apt to end up either with three different Gods, each with a particular agenda, or with one God who functions in three different ways but is not a triune God of three Persons.

Beyond that, if we leave Christ out of the story of creation, then we risk creating a great gap between creation and salvation. In extreme form, this danger becomes the heresy of Marcion who, in the second century, said that there were two different Gods: an evil, or at least incompetent, one who made the physical universe, and the loving Father of Christ, who rescued us from the world the first God had made. We risk some analogous mistake if we make Christ a redeemer who had nothing to do with creation.

We believe instead that Christ does not come into the world as a stranger in a strange land. "Long ago God spoke to our ancestors in many and various ways by the prophets, but in these last days he has spoken to us by a Son, whom he appointed heir of all things, through whom he also created the worlds" (Heb. 1:1–2). The world may not recognize Christ, but "the world came into being through him. . . . He came to what was his own" (John 1:10–11). As Athanasius wrote in the fourth century, "The renewal of creation has been the work of the self-same Word that made it at the beginning."[2] The very structure of this Statement tries to convey that point: beginning with Christ and then turning to creation reminds us that it is the God known in Jesus Christ who created all things.

Similarly, when the Holy Spirit moves in our hearts and lives, that Spirit is not fighting against the grain of creation but working to bring about creation as it was meant to be, a creation infused with that Spirit from its beginning. (See line 53.) When Genesis speaks of the Spirit that swept over the face of the waters, Calvin said, it reminds us

> not only that the beauty of the universe (which we now perceive) owes its strength and preservation to the power of the Spirit but that before this adornment was added, even then the Spirit was occupied with tending that confused mass. . . . For it is the Spirit who, everywhere diffused, sustains all things, causes them to grow, and quickens them in heaven and in earth. (*Institutes* 1.13.14)

In sovereign love God created the world. The main reason to talk about creation is not to try to explain when or how things all began long ago, but to get clear on some truths about the world we live in right now. The doctrine of creation implies that the universe belongs to God, who made it, and this has at least two important implications. First, if God made the universe, then it is good, it is not a maze without a plan, but has a purpose, and we can ask about the purpose of our lives within it. Second, if the universe belongs to God, then it does not belong to us. In Jürgen Moltmann's fine phrase, "Nature must no longer be viewed as 'unclaimed property.' "[3] There are, of course, good selfish reasons for us human beings to take care of our environment, so that we do not choke on our own waste, but Christian faith teaches that we have responsibilities to the rest of the world that reach beyond its impact on us. In the Genesis story, after all, God sees the light and the land and the water and the living creatures as "good" even before human beings are created. The world is not ours to do with as we please; it has an Owner with a right to demand an accounting from the tenants.

God is not yet finished with the universe—far from it. God continues to care for creation and keeps making new things happen, creating new things. This Statement, however, uses the past tense of the verb, "created." That verb tense emphasizes the irrevocability of God's act of creation. God created out of pure love—no necessity to be obeyed, no lack to be filled. But now God has created a universe and called it good. When we trust in God as creator, we trust that God will not change opinion, decide that the whole idea of creation was a mistake, and return to solitude or try again. There are new things, some of them full of surprises, yet to come, but God will not go back on the act of creation; in that sense creation has happened once and for all.

In sovereign love God created the world good. Whatever distortions, corruptions, and conflict may emerge in this world, whatever damage we may do to it, our world comes from God, all of it, beautiful and full of wonders. "There is no spot in the universe wherein you cannot discern at least some sparks of his glory" (Calvin, *Institutes* 1.5.1).

Too many Christians have treated the physical as if it were evil, something from which we ought to escape. Such ideas are prominent in some strands of Greek thought—the Neoplatonic philosopher Plotinus dreamed of freeing his soul, "liberation from the alien that besets us here, a life taking no pleasure in the things of the earth," and one of his students remarked that he "seemed ashamed of being in the body."[4] But this is not the dominant biblical view. God saw that the world "was very good" (Gen. 1:31). We may misuse our bodies, but they are good, every part of them, part of what God has given us. We may misuse and abuse the resources of the natural world, but the pleasures they bring us are not in themselves evil, but good gifts from God.

Calvin said that food was created "not only to provide for necessity but also for delight and good cheer" (*Institutes* 3.10.2). God gives us not only water to quench our thirst but wine to gladden the heart and "to make us merry."[5] "God has clothed the flowers with the great beauty that greets our eyes, the sweetness of smell that is wafted upon our nostrils. . . . Did he not, in short, render many things attractive to us apart from their necessary use?" (*Institutes* 3.10.2). We should live moderately and share with our neighbors, and avoid wasting the good things God has given us. But, at the same time, let us enjoy and be grateful. This is a world God made good, and it is no honor to the maker to despise the work of the craft. So Augustine imagined searching for an understanding of God:

> And what is this God? I asked the earth and it answered: "I am not he," and all things that are on the earth confessed the same. I asked the sea and deeps and the creeping things with living souls, and they replied, "We are not your God. Look above us." . . . I asked the heaven, the sun, the moon, the stars, and "No," they said, "we are not the God for whom you are looking." And I said to all those things which stand about the gates of my senses: "Tell me about my God, you who are not He. Tell me something about Him." And they cried out in a low voice: "He made us." My question was in my contemplation of them, and their answer was in their beauty.[6]

When we manage to notice the beauty of God's creation, that can be one way in which we praise God. Seeing God's power and goodness in creation increases our trust in God, and admiration leads to gratitude, and gratitude leads to seeking to serve.

> Whenever we call God the Creator of heaven and earth [Calvin writes,] let us at the same time bear in mind that the dispensation of all those things which he has made is in his own hand and power and that we are indeed his children. . . . So, invited by the great sweetness of his beneficence and goodness, let us study to love and serve him with all our heart. (*Institutes* 1.14.22)

The God who created all things *makes* us human beings *in God's image*[7]: "Then God said, 'Let us make humankind in our image, according to our likeness'" (Gen. 1:26–27). What does that mean? Starting with Irenaeus in the second century and all through the Middle Ages, many Christian theologians tried to make a distinction between "image" and "likeness." The "image," they said, consisted in our basic human freedom and rationality; the "likeness" was the relation we had with God. Sin destroyed the likeness, but not the image. Luther, however, and most of the Protestant tradition following him, denied this distinction. First, Luther recognized in this passage in Genesis the parallel structure characteristic of Hebrew poetry, which tends to repeat the same thought in slightly different words. One should therefore not look for a different meaning the second time around. Even more than that, Luther said, we are not first of all human and then in some kind of relationship with God—our relation to God defines the most basic character of our humanity. "Image" and "likeness" represent two different ways of pointing to that same relationship.

But what is that relationship? The Christian tradition has never produced a single "official" answer to that question. The Scots Confession, for instance, points to a number of ways in which human beings might be like God: in "wisdom, lordship, justice, free will, and self-consciousness" (3.02). Other theologians have suggested that we are like God in *substance* (our souls are immortal), in *proportionality* (just as God has dominion over all things, so God has given human beings dominion over the rest of our world), or in *relation* (the community of human beings with each other corresponds to the fellowship of the Persons of God in the Trinity).[8]

For the sake of exploring what it can mean that we are made in God's image, it may be worth exploring in a bit more detail a few themes that often appear. Consider our *freedom*, our *knowing,* and our *loving*.

We do not have the kind of absolute *freedom* that God has. God creates with no prior rules at all, while our choices always take place in a context where much has already been decided. But we do make choices. The grass will be grass and the birds will follow their nature come what may. We choose what to make of our lives; we even have the capacity, in sin, to start to turn away from what it is to be human. In that partial capacity to define our own selves, we are a bit like God.

Our *knowing* is also not exactly like God's knowing. It is, just for a start, always limited and imperfect.

> For as the heavens are higher than the earth,
>   so are my ways higher than your ways
>   and my thoughts higher than your thoughts.
>   (Isa. 55:9)

But still, we can understand something of the world around us. "Man is but a reed, the most feeble thing in nature," Pascal wrote in the seventeenth century, "but he is a thinking reed. . . . A vapor, a drop of water suffices to kill him. But, if the universe were to crush him, man would still be more noble than that which killed him, because he knows that he dies; . . . the universe knows nothing of this."[9] Frail creatures that we are, tiny specks on a minor planet, we can come up with theories that encompass the whole universe in understanding, that see it, however imperfectly, as a single whole, and in doing that we image just a bit the God who made that universe.

Third and finally, we can be *loving*. We never love quite the way God does. God needs nothing, and loves in pure selflessness. Our needs and desires always get mixed together with the love we have for others. But we can really love, in our limited and imperfect fashion, and in that love too we form an image of the loving God who made us. As Gregory of Nyssa wrote in the fourth century, "For the life of the Supreme Being is love . . . and humanity is, in a way, like God, as bearing within itself some resemblance to its Prototype."[10]

We are not God, but as free, knowing, loving creatures we are creatures in God's image. Focusing on freedom, knowledge, and love, to be sure, directs our attention to the human mind. Human beings have bodies too! In Calvin's time, the Lutheran theologian Andreas Osiander had proposed that human beings were in the image of God because, unlike the animals who bend to the ground, we walk upright, with our eyes on the heavens. Calvin thought this was a bit silly, but he conceded there might be something in it. After all, our bodies are part of who we are, and therefore it is important—even if there seems little value in getting more specific—if *we* are in the image of God, to say that in some way even "our outward form . . . more closely joins us to God" (*Institutes* 1.15.3).

What matters most, though, is that we *are* made in God's image. Every part of creation manifests God's glory, but we human beings are special: we can see and understand that glory; we can return a measure of love in loving God, and we can freely choose to do this. "God created man good and in his image, that is, in true righteousness and holiness, so that he might rightly know God his Creator, love him with his whole heart, and live with him in eternal blessedness, praising and glorifying him" (Heidelberg Catechism 4.006).

Moreover, we are made *equally in God's image, male and female, of every race and people.* A long and sad tradition of Christian thought has acknowledged that all human beings are made in the image of God, but insisted that some—usually males, or whites—are made *more* in the image of God than others. In the sixth century the Council of Macon, after lengthy debate, affirmed that women did indeed have souls, but by one vote only. H. Shelton Smith entitled a fine book on racism in the Christian tradition *In His Image, But* . . . .[11] This Statement of Faith wants to eliminate all those "buts."

> So God created humankind in his image,
>   in the image of God he created them;
>   male and female he created them.
>   (Gen. 1:27)

Male and female, all humankind, unambiguously and equally made in God's image.

In all kinds of ways, of course, we are *not* all equal. Some of us are stronger, some of us are smarter, some of us seem to have more patience or a greater capacity for love and compassion. Some "excel in keenness; others are superior in judgment; still others have a readier wit to learn this or that art. In this variety God commends his grace to us, lest anyone should claim as his own what flowed from the sheer bounty of God" (*Institutes* 2.2.17). No doubt we develop some of these differences by our own efforts, but some of the distinctions do seem inborn. In that sense, we are not made *equal.*

But we are made *equally in God's image.* And, compared with that, all those other inequalities seem remarkably unimportant. The experience of some families with children with Down's syndrome comes to mind as an example. The rest of us often sympathize with their misfortune, and the burdens and the challenges they face are indeed very real. But sometimes they remind the rest of us of the great joy that they meet in this special, loving human person who is a part of their family. They teach us in a particularly dramatic way the unimportance of all the ways in which we are unequal in the face of our basic equality as human beings, an equality we affirm when we say that we are all made equally in the image of God.

In our time, many Christians have come to a growing sense of how important it is to emphasize that equality. Too much of racism and sexism and other kinds of prejudice has been able to "appeal" to the Christian tradition for "support." We need to affirm unambiguously that such appeals distort the message of the Christian gospel. They hurt people who are persecuted and demeaned. They also hurt people who are made to feel superior, made to feel that they are better than others, and are thereby left in a state of dangerous misunderstanding of their state as sinners before God.

Still, it is not enough to say that we have all been made equally in the image of God. We might be made to live our lives equal but separate. Reformed Christianity, however, teaches that as human beings we are made to live *in community,* indeed to live *as one community.*

Some of the noblest human insights of the world into which Christianity came proclaimed that human beings ought to seek individual self-sufficiency. "Let him then who wishes to be free not wish for anything or avoid anything that depends on others," the Stoic philosopher Epictetus wrote, "or else he is bound to be a slave."[12] That was not and is not the point of view of Christianity. We believe that human beings were made for community. We see in Jesus Christ, who lived the whole of life for others, the model of what it is to be fully human. We believe ourselves to be made in the image of a triune God, in which three Persons are one in perfect, mutual love. Christianity does not teach people to be self-sufficient.

Too often, however, human communities define themselves by including some and excluding others, by distinguishing between "us" and "them." Christians believe that all humanity was created to live as *one* community. In the Genesis story, God made humanity as a single family. After the Flood, the biblical story tells us, God again sought to populate the world from one family. But the descendants of Noah could not accept their status as creatures. They would not trust God to sustain them. They sought to build a tower to heaven, in part out of fear that otherwise they would be "scattered abroad upon the face of the whole earth" (Gen. 11:4). But their lack of trust, their prideful attempt to base everything on their own accomplishments, led to the realization of their worst fears—their language confused and divided, they were scattered over all the earth.

The story makes at least two points. First, the human community is divided only as the consequence of sin; we were *made* to *live as* one *community*. Second, the form of that sin is our unwillingness to trust in God to be the foundation of our community, putting our trust instead in ourselves or in the strength of some human group or institution. The book of Revelation imagines "the holy city Jerusalem *coming down* out of heaven *from God*" (Rev. 21:10, emphasis added). The folly of the Babelites was to think they could build their own way up to heaven.

Sin continues to divide and distort human communities, but we do occasionally catch glimpses of what a better world might be. On Pentecost the earliest church experienced, miraculously, the beginning of a kind of reversal of Babel. "All of them were filled with the Holy Spirit and began to speak in other languages, as the Spirit gave them ability" (Acts 2:4). With the help of the Spirit, we in the church are charged with continuing to try to do that: to show what a human community would be like without sin, and without all the barriers sin creates. We often don't do it very well, but we need to keep trying.

> Do not lie to one another, seeing that you have stripped off the old self with its practices and have clothed yourselves with the new self, which is being renewed in knowledge according to the image of its creator. In that renewal there is no longer Greek and Jew, circumcised and uncircumcised, barbarian, Scythian, slave and free; but Christ is all and in all! (Col. 3:9–11)

If we are made for community, we are made for community open to all humankind, for we all share the image of God. Our faith does not call us to live "separate but equal." "The image of God," Calvin wrote, "ought to be a bond of holy union among us" (*Institutes* 1.15.4). "There are many apparently liberal, who yet do not feel for the miseries of their brethren."[13] But their failure is a form of sin, for God intended humanity for "the bonds of mutual society, hence they must mutually perform good offices for each other. Here, then, it is required of the rich to succor the poor, and to offer bread to the hungry."[14]

The "Declaration of Faith for the Church in South Africa," adopted in revised form by the Presbyterian Church of Southern Africa in 1981, declares:

> We believe in God the Father,
> who created all the world,
> who will unite all things in Christ
> and who wants all people to live together
>   as brothers and sisters in one family.[15]

It takes courage to confess that faith in South Africa today. The words may come more easily for us, but we need to face honestly the ways in which they would often challenge us too if we took them seriously.

8. Sin
(Lines 33–39)

33 But we rebel against God; we hide from our Creator.
34   Ignoring God's commandments,
35   we violate the image of God in others and ourselves,
36   accept lies as truth,
37   exploit neighbor and nature,
38   and threaten death to the planet entrusted to our care.
39   We deserve God's condemnation.

Look around: Look at abused children running away from home to live on the streets of great cities, choosing between hunger and prostitution; look at wars where famine serves both sides as a weapon; look at the hate in the eyes of a racist and the darkness in the eyes of a murderer; look at wives abused and women raped; look at AIDS victims dying in a quarantine of fear; look at waste and pollution and the juxtaposition of great wealth and abject poverty; look at the whole sad chronicle of human history, and all the trivial ways in which, every day, we hurt our neighbors or turn away from their need in indifference.

It has been said that sin is the one Christian doctrine for which there is incontrovertible empirical evidence, and so it might seem. But we human beings have an amazing capacity for denying the obvious. We are good at finding excuses. We see the wickedness in the world, but often not in *our* political cause, *our* nation, *our* church, ourselves. "Man never achieves a clear knowledge of himself unless he has first looked upon God's face," Calvin wrote. "For we always seem to ourselves righteous and upright and wise and holy—this pride is innate in all of us" (*Institutes* 1.1.2). As Christians, it is only when we have grasped that God's creation is good and that we are made in God's image, and above all only when we have seen in Christ how much God loves us and what human beings were truly meant to be, that we realize the full actuality of our sin.

Many of us, as we grow up, get in the habit of thinking of "sin" primarily as something we do as individuals, in our private lives. "Sin" has to do, we think, with sexual misconduct, or drinking too much, or lying to parents or friends. Such sins can be real, and serious, but they are not the only form sin can take. We also sin in our public lives and through the groups and institutions to which we belong. If Christians remain silent when their governments engage in despicable behavior, or belong to clubs that practice discrimination, or pass up ways of influencing the companies for which they work when those companies are cheating customers or taking advantage of migrant workers or polluting the environment—that too is a form of sin.

The authors of the Bible rarely tried to "explain" the origin of sin; indeed, they recognized that the origin of sin cannot be explained. If some force "caused" us to sin, we would not be responsible. We *choose* sin, and that choice seems deeply irrational. Why would people created by a good God, who loves them and showers them with benefits, deliberately turn away from that God, start hating each other, and deny their own natures? Yet wherever we look in humanity, high and low, in every human place, we see sin.

Many Christian theologians have sought to explain that universality of sin by talking about "original sin," but they have explained that sin and our relation to it in varied ways. Augustine thought it was a kind of genetic inheritance passed down from Adam and Eve. Some modern theologians have explained it in social terms—growing up in a corrupt society, we cannot help becoming corrupt—or in terms of psychological development—by the time our reason develops enough to make the moral law clear to us, we have all already been led astray by our desires. The dominant account in Calvin and in the Reformed confessions (and, for that matter, the view Paul seems to take in Romans 5) emphasizes Adam's *representative* character: "The Lord deposited with Adam the gifts He chose to confer on human nature. Therefore, when he lost that which he had received, he lost them not only for himself but also for us" (*Institutes* 2.1.7). Adam's sin is "imputed" to the rest of us (Westminster Confession 6.033). The Second Helvetic Confession (5.037), however, and sometimes Calvin himself[1] follow Augustine in describing a kind of genetic inheritance. In short, there is no consistent or official Reformed explanation of the mechanism of original sin.

Calvin and nearly all his contemporaries thought of "Adam" and "Eve" as particular historical individuals. Such a belief seems hard to reconcile with the conclusions of modern science, and perhaps it does not fit the meaning of the text itself very well either. In Hebrew, "Adam" means "human being" and "Eve" means "mother," and in a way the story seems to be about each one of us. That is often the way Calvin himself read it in practice. As with the creation story that precedes it, it can be only after we realize that the story is not "history" that we realize most fully how true it is.

What matters about this story of "original sin" is that sin is not something into which some of us happen to fall. "All we like sheep have gone astray" (Isa. 53:6). "If we search the remotest past, I say that none of the saints . . . has attained to that goal of love so as to love God 'with all his heart, all his mind, all his soul, and all his strength' " (*Institutes* 2.7.5). We are all sinners. To sin is not our nature, for we are God's creatures and, as such, good. But the human reality we know is a reality of universal sin. As we confess our faith as Christians, we do not pretend to be free of sin, or to hope that we might be, or to identify human individuals or institutions or ideals that are without sin—we *confess* our sin. We turn to the grace of Christ not because the road out of sin looks a bit difficult, but because by our own efforts there is no road out of sin.

And yet, that sin is freely chosen. While *every* human being chooses sin, still every human being really *chooses* sin. As a character in William Faulkner's *Requiem for a Nun* puts the paradox of sin: "You ain't *got* to. You can't help it."[2] Both sides of the paradox are important to Christian faith—the inevitable universality of sin ("You can't help it"), and our responsibility for sin always freely chosen ("You ain't got to"). Stated like that, it does seem a paradox. But it corresponds to our experience as Christians: We know ourselves to be judged guilty in a way that makes sense only if we are responsible for our actions; we also know the sheer inevitability of human sin.

In the story of Adam and Eve, Genesis tells about the eating of some fruit. But the fruit is not the point of the story. As Calvin says, "To regard Adam's sin as gluttonous intemperance . . . is childish" (*Institutes* 2.1.4). It is hard to settle on a single word to define that first sin as the story describes it. Since our faith begins in trust, perhaps sin begins with *distrust*. "Did God say . . . ?" the crafty serpent asks, and plants a doubt amid what had until that moment remained trusting confidence. Since sin involves a refusal to accept our role as creatures, perhaps it begins in *disobedience*. God lays down only one rule in the midst of the garden's abundance, and human beings promptly disobey it. Or again, there is *pride*—the creature just made out of the dust of the ground wants to put itself in the place of God.

We human beings *rebel against God*. Distrusting the relation we have with God, we disobediently try to reject our creaturehood and proudly try to put ourselves in God's place. As Augustine put it, "Man regards himself in his own light, and turns away from that light which would make a man himself a light if he would set his heart to it."[3] We are like tenants who claim someone else's land as if it were our own, then murder the servants the owner sends to collect the rent (Matt. 21:33–39; see also Lev. 25:23–24). We are like the prodigal son, who cannot accept living in his father's house but asks for his inheritance, in cash, to go off and live independently and spend it as he chooses (Luke 15:11–13).

The rebellion takes many forms. We try to acquire so much power or wealth that we will be secure, on our own, regardless of what happens, and in so doing we try to make ourselves God—as if we could trust in ourselves rather than needing to put our trust in God. We implicitly claim that we are so virtuous that we can win salvation on our own and do not need God's help. We set ourselves up as if we could decide for ourselves the purposes of our lives, as if we were the masters of our fates and the captains of our souls.

Sometimes, on the other hand, we concede that we are not, as individuals, so special, but start to worship "my country, right or wrong," or "my family, the center of everything for me," or "this cause of mine, for which I would do anything, sacrifice anything." We set them up as idols in the place of God. But they too are part of God's creation. Nothing but God is God, and every attempt to put something else in God's place rebels against God.

We are creatures made in the image of God. Sometimes we try to deny that we are creatures. But sometimes we do not accept that we are made in God's image. *We hide from our Creator.*

> At times we seek in pride to become gods,
> denying the good limits that define us as creatures.
> At other times we draw back in apathy,
> refusing to fulfill our human responsibilities.[4]

Adam and Eve hide themselves from the presence of the Lord (Gen. 3:8). The prophet Jonah receives a call to go and preach to Nineveh and tries to run away. Called to proclaim the word of the Lord to Pharaoh, Moses protests, "I have never been eloquent . . . I am slow of speech and slow of tongue. . . . O my Lord, please send someone else" (Ex. 4:10, 13).

In the passage just quoted, A Declaration of Faith called this sin "apathy," Karl Barth called it "sloth," Reinhold Niebuhr named it "sensuality." Whatever word we use, hiding ourselves from God is the sin of trying to be less than we really are.

That sin can take dramatic forms. We can turn to drink or drugs as a way of hiding from challenges and responsibilities. Some people manage to destroy their whole lives in hiding. But often it takes more modest forms. I could go back to school and perhaps start a new career, but, well, I just never get around to it. It's flattering that you ask me to serve on a church committee, but I've never done that before, and I don't think I want to try. Somebody really ought to do something about these local problems, but no one would listen to someone like me, so what's the use? We even claim all this as virtue—Christian humility, we may call it—and do not recognize it as the sin of failing to realize fully what we might be as creatures made in God's image. Women writing theology have recently helped us see this other kind of sin more clearly, for in our culture it is often women who have found it more tempting.[5] Our society pushes men toward pride—toward ambition, career, "macho" toughness. But it has often encouraged women to "hide"—to live exclusively through their husbands and children, not to develop their own talents. Preaching that unrelievedly denounced pride might have been the message that men needed to hear, but too often it reinforced women in their sin of "hiding."

Stereotypes, of course, are always dangerous. Men and women both commit all kinds of sins. For that matter, these sins, which might seem opposites, can turn out to have odd connections. When we seem to be most arrogant, we can in fact be feeling most insecure; in Reinhold Niebuhr's wonderful phrase, "there is no level of greatness and power in which the lash of fear is not at least one strand in the whip of ambition."[6] And the refusal to take a risk can sometimes grow out of a pride that will not risk failure. The important point is that *both* ways of denying what God made us to be—whether setting ourselves up as gods and denying our creaturehood or denying our real abilities and potentials—both are really sins.

Sin leads to *ignoring God's commandments*—and ignoring God's commandments is itself further sin. When we are no longer in right relationship with God, we stop paying attention to what God wants us to do.

"What is sin?" asks Question 14 of the Westminster Shorter Catechism. "Sin is any want of conformity unto, or transgression of, the law of God" (7.014). The Heidelberg Catechism addresses the same point, only slightly differently:

Q. 3. Where do you learn of your sin and its wretched consequences?

A. From the Law of God.

Q. 4. What does the Law of God require of us?

A. Jesus Christ teaches this in summary in Matthew

22:37–40: "You shall love the Lord your God with all
your heart, and with all your soul, and with all your
mind. This is the great and first commandment. And a
second is like it, you shall love your neighbor as yourself.
On these two commandments depend all the law and the
prophets." (4.003–4.004)

"Legalism" is a negative word. None of us much likes taking orders. And one of the themes of Paul's theology certainly
seems to be that in Christ we are set free from the law. But
Christian freedom stands in a complicated relationship to
God's commandments. Some of the rules we encounter in our
lives are arbitrary, but some seem just part of the nature of
things. You cannot learn calculus without working through
some sample problems; you cannot keep alert indefinitely without a good night's sleep. Rules like that are not arbitrarily imposed by math teachers or parents. They flow out of the nature
of calculus or the human animal.

God's commandments have more in common with that
kind of rule. If we stop loving God, we are cut off from God. If
we stop loving our neighbors, we isolate ourselves in hatred. If
we disobey the commandments, we stop being the kind of
creatures we were meant to be. One lie leads to another; every
sin makes it that much harder to resist temptation. God does
not need to seek us out to punish us when we disobey: we simply suffer the natural consequences of our disobedience.

In contrast, obedience to God's commandments properly
understood does not feel like constraint but like freedom, like
living as we were meant to live. After all, we do not complain
that playing baseball or writing a sonnet involves rules, and
rules constrain us. We could not play baseball or write a sonnet
at all without the rules that create a structure which opens up
the possibility of a new activity. So it is within the structure of
God's commandments that we find the possibility of a free
human life.

The role of God's law in the Christian life has always been
an important feature of the Reformed tradition. The Lutheran
branch of the Reformation characteristically emphasized the
contrast between law and gospel. The gospel, they said, freed

us from the law. The law primarily serves only two functions: (1) it convicts us of our sins by showing us how far we would fail apart from grace; (2) it sufficiently threatens sinners to preserve a kind of order in society.

Calvin and others in the Reformed tradition, however, identified a *third* use of the law, a much more positive one: The law gives us positive guidance in living a Christian life. It helps us know how we should live our lives, and it gives us encouragement in following the pattern it describes.

> Here is the best instrument for them to learn more thoroughly each day the nature of the Lord's will to which they aspire. . . . Again, because we need not only teaching but also exhortation, the servant of God will also avail himself of this benefit of the law: by frequent meditation upon it to be aroused to obedience, be strengthened by it, and be drawn back from the slippery path of transgression. (*Institutes* 2.7.12)

We are created as free, knowing, and loving creatures, made in God's image (see line 30). When we sin, we lose our freedom, we distort our understanding, and we turn from love to hate and envy and bitterness. *We violate the image of God in others and ourselves.*

If freedom lies in obedience, then disobedience leads to slavery. "Everyone who commits sin is a slave to sin" (John 8:34). The drug addict is but one extreme form of the universal pattern of sin: Addicts begin by freely choosing, and at each choice lose a bit more of their freedom until they find themselves entrapped by the consequences of their own choosing. So it is with jealousy or greed or sexual excess or any other kind of sin. Trapped in sin, we can only say with Paul, "I can will what is right, but I cannot do it. For I do not do the good I want, but the evil I do not want is what I do" (Rom. 7:18–19).

Further, gone astray in sin, we cannot understand the world aright. "Ever since the creation of the world [God's] eternal power and divine nature, invisible though they are, have been understood and seen through the things he has made" (Rom. 1:20). But we get so caught up in our sin that we cannot see the wonder of God's creation. "However much the glory of

God shines forth, scarcely one man in a hundred is true specta-
tor of it" (*Institutes* 1.5.8). But it is more than that. How
often, looking back, we realize what we should have done. If
only I had apologized! If only I had taken a little more time to
listen! If what I should have done is so obvious, why did I fail
to see it? In sin we are blinded, just as we are trapped. We lose
our understanding, just as we lose our freedom. And we also
lose our capacity to love. Envy and spitefulness take over our
lives.

It may seem odd to talk about sinning against the image of
God in ourselves. We are apt to say, "Why was that wrong? I
didn't hurt anyone else." Often enough, the claim is a lie.
Those who waste away their lives often cause great pain to
those around them. The gifts they might have exercised to the
benefit of their neighbors lie fallow. But more than that, the
creatures they might have been, glorifying God by their own
particular excellence, go unrealized. So it is not just our business and no one else's, for we are not our own, but God's.

Of course we violate the image of God in others as well. The
human beings in need whom we ignore or treat with contempt,
every one of them is made in God's image. If we casually dismiss
the consequences in human suffering of our plans, if we treat
someone as a sexual object to be used for our pleasure, then we
are violating the image of God. " 'Lord, when was it that we saw
you hungry or thirsty or a stranger or naked or sick or in prison,
and did not take care of you?' Then he will answer them, 'Truly
I tell you, just as you did not do it to one of the least of these,
you did not do it to me.' " (Matt. 25:44–45). "No one can be
injurious to his brother," Calvin once wrote, "without wound-
ing God himself."[7]

Our sins of violating the image of God often lead us to
falsehood. *We accept lies as truth.* Lying, indeed, seems part of
the nature of sin. When the devil lies, "he speaks according to
his own nature, for he is a liar and the father of lies" (John
8:44). Those who drink too much and abuse their families lie
about the drink and the abuse. National officials lie about a
policy they have adopted and its consequences. Polluters lie
about the effects of their factories' emissions. And so it goes.
"Speeding, officer? I don't think I was driving over fifty-five."

The lie comes almost automatically off the tongue. Cain murders his brother, and as soon as God asks him, "Where is your brother Abel?" replies, "I do not know; am I my brother's keeper?" (Gen. 4:9).

Reinhold Niebuhr once remarked that such lies were a kind of evidence that we are not *totally* depraved. Even in our sin, we can tell enough of what is right and wrong that we instinctively deny the reality of what we have done.[8] That, at least, is a good sign.

But most of what there is about lying is not good. We lie to each other, and every lie makes honesty more difficult. We lie to ourselves, and we try to lie to God. It is not surprising that lies should be connected with sin, for sin rests on pretending that we don't need God, on putting ourselves in the place of God—both based in falsehood. We have "exchanged the truth about God for a lie and worshiped and served the creature rather than the Creator" (Rom. 1:25).

When sinners "serve the creature," however, we do not help others and care for God's creation. Instead, we exploit *neighbor and nature.* Jesus cared for others. He "came not to be served but to serve" (Matt. 20:28). He marveled at the beauty of the lilies of the field. When we sin, we try to think how we can get *others* to serve *us.* We wonder if there could be some way to make a profit off those lilies. We "exploit neighbor and nature."

The exploitation of neighbors is a very old story, already familiar in the time of ancient Israel. Amos denounced those who

> sell the righteous for silver,
>   and the needy for a pair of sandals—
> they who trample the head of the poor into the dust of the earth,
>   and push the afflicted out of the way.
>
> (Amos 2:6–7)

In our time too, wealth and success can rest on exploitation of others. Sometimes the connection is obvious and direct, as when we have cheated someone else out of what was properly hers or his. But other times we have come by what is ours honestly enough, except that we have in abundance, and someone else is going hungry.

The Reformed tradition has taught that that too is exploitation. Calvin addressed such issues in commenting on the Ten Commandments. In the commandment "You shall not kill," he wrote, "men's common sense will see only that we must abstain from wronging anyone or desiring to do so. Besides this, it contains, I say, the requirement that we give our neighbor's life all the help we can" (*Institutes* 2.8.46).

Q.107. Is it enough, then, if we do not kill our neighbor . . . ?

A. No; for when God condemns envy, hatred, and anger, he requires us to love our neighbor as ourselves, to show patience, peace, gentleness, mercy, and friendliness toward him, to prevent injury as much as we can, also to do good to our enemies.

He forbids not only the theft and robbery which civil authorities punish, but God also labels as theft all wicked tricks and schemes by which we seek to get for ourselves our neighbor's goods, whether by force or under pretext of right, such as false weights and measures, deceptive advertising or merchandising, counterfeit money, exorbitant interest, or any other means forbidden by God. He also forbids all greed and misuse and waste of his gifts. (Heidelberg Catechism 4.107, 4.110)

So we are exploiting our neighbors not just when we cheat and steal but when we fail to do what we can to help them. And in a complicated and interconnected world, that does not mean just the people I meet on the street—my "neighbors" include people half a world away who are affected by my actions or the way I live my life.

One of the ways many of us in wealthier countries affect the whole world is by taking far more than our share of its goods, or by doing far more than our share of damage to it. We exploit nature as well as neighbor. In a world shared by all humanity and belonging to God, we may use so many resources for our own luxuries that there are not enough to go around, or the beauty and health of God's world are threatened.

The Reformed tradition has something very clear to say about that kind of sin. In literature and popular image, the

"Calvinist" or the "Puritan" has often had a bad press—dour, frugal, grim, "haunted by the fear that some people, somewhere, may be enjoying themselves." No doubt any caricature has an element of truth; joy and spontaneity have not always been the hallmarks of our particular tradition. But that caricature may also point to some significant virtues. At its best, the Reformed tradition calls people to a life of moderation and responsibility: not to be wasteful, not to be greedy, not to be dishonest in one's dealings; to use what we have sensibly, and share it with others.

Calvin himself laid down three rules for how we should use the goods given to us. We are not required, he said, to give up everything we have and live in poverty. *But*:

1. "If we have riches, we should not put our heart or confidence in them. . . . We should be ready to give them up when that seems good to God."

2. "We should work with integrity . . . [and] go briskly about our business with honesty."

3. "Whoever has a great deal should not misuse it by squandering it . . . or by [acquiring] superfluous things out of pride and vanity. Rather, by using it moderately he should employ the property that has been given to him in order to help and to provide for his neighbors, seeing himself as God's steward who possesses the goods that he has on condition that he must one day render an account."[9]

The dour old Calvinist in a black coat may have been a grim miser, but on the other hand may have been avoiding extravagance in dress and life in order to avoid the need to seek vast wealth, or in order to have more to give to the poor. Perhaps in our time more than ever we could profitably think about the virtues of a Reformed style of life, a life of simplicity, honesty, generosity, and prudent stewardship of God's gifts.

The ancient law codes in Leviticus made such matters very concrete: "When you reap the harvest of your land, you shall not reap to the very edges of your field, or gather the gleanings of your harvest. You shall not strip your vineyard bare, or gather the fallen grapes of your vineyard; you shall leave them for the poor and the alien: I am the Lord your God" (Lev. 19:9–10). Hebrew farmers were called to not squeeze every possible profit out of the land, and their moderation was to provide for the poor and the outsider.

It is good advice for Reformed Christians, and not just for those of us who farm the land, either. We need to think imaginatively about the equivalent for our time of the Levitical laws of harvest, ways of living and working that share with our neighbors and respect our land.

Such concerns are especially important in our time, when our sin could *threaten death to the planet entrusted to our care.* Human beings have always polluted and wasted and ignored and hacked away at God's creation. But for most of human history, there were modest limits to the damage we could do. Modern technology and the sheer expansion of the human population keep increasing our power to harm. The words of the prophet Hosea have new meaning for us:

> There is no faithfulness or loyalty,
> and no knowledge of God in the land.
> . . . .
>
> Therefore the land mourns,
> and all who live in it languish;
> together with the wild animals
> and the birds of the air,
> even the fish of the sea are perishing.
> (Hos. 4:1, 3)

A nuclear war could fundamentally alter life on the planet; trends of global warming may already be doing so. Sailors report serious evidence of pollution in the most isolated stretches of midocean. "We face today the growing crisis of the destruction of nature (and therefore of the ground of our life) arising from the relentless population explosion, from unrestrained human greed and extravagance and from the misuse of knowledge."[10]

The potential harm, then, is new, but the problem is old, and the responsibility is old. God put the first human being in the Garden of Eden "to till it and keep it" (Gen. 2:15). The

Hebrew word for "till" can also mean "serve" and connotes respect, even reverence, and the word for "keep" suggests an act of protection or caring, not just possession. We are given a responsibility, a job to do. When we ignore that responsibility, when we waste what God has given us, then we are sinning. We will not destroy God; we will not destroy God's creation—overstating our power for evil could be just another form of pride. But we could destroy ourselves. We could turn much of this planet, rich with life, into a place of death.

In short, *we deserve God's condemnation*. This line summarizes this section, the confession of sin in lines 33–39. Our sin poisons our lives, it harms others, it endangers God's good creation, but above all it deserves God's condemnation. Sin is not the way God wants us to live; it is not the way God meant us to live. From forgetting that, all the lies and all the distortions and all the disastrous consequences follow inevitably.

This concluding line changed several times in the drafting of the statement. An early draft circulated to the churches generated a good many complaints about the word "condemnation." "I do not believe in a God who condemns," several people said. So the drafting committee changed the line to "We deserve God's judgment." But the Standing Committee of the 1989 General Assembly recommended changing it back to "condemnation," and so it stayed. For one thing, "judgment" seems ambiguous: we can receive a judgment that finds us innocent. And surely here we want a word just as strong as we can find—no excuses, no half measures, nothing short of the acknowledgment of the full reality of our sin.

The critics made an important point, but I think they misread the line. God does *not* condemn. But we do *deserve* condemnation—a different point altogether.

> "There is no one who is righteous, not even one;
>> there is no one who has understanding,
>>> there is no one who seeks God.
> All have turned aside, together they have become worthless;
>> there is no one who shows kindness,
>>> there is not even one."

(Rom. 3:10–12)

We want to protest and insist that we are not quite that bad. The confession of sin is a painful business. But it can also be liberating. We do not have to try to prove that somehow we do not deserve God's condemnation. God does not condemn us, but that is because of God's love, not our merit. When we can stop pretending, stop trying to justify ourselves, stop making excuses, we can feel newly honest and free.

9. Covenant
(Lines 40–51)

40   Yet God acts with justice and mercy to redeem creation.
41   In everlasting love,
42   the God of Abraham and Sarah chose a covenant people
43   to bless all families of the earth.
44   Hearing their cry,
45   God delivered the children of Israel
46   from the house of bondage.
47   Loving us still,
48   God makes us heirs with Christ of the covenant.
49   Like a mother who will not forsake her nursing child,
50   like a father who runs to welcome the prodigal home,
51   God is faithful still.

Yet. . . One presentation to the 1990 General Assembly, during the debate on this Brief Statement of Faith, pointed to this as the single most important word in the Statement. Though we are faithless, yet God remains faithful. When we are enslaved, yet God hears our cries. "While we still were sinners Christ died for us" (Rom. 5:8). When we say that we deserve God's condemnation, *the very next thing* that needs to be said begins with, "Yet . . ."

Yet God acts with justice and mercy to redeem creation. The God of Christian faith, the God of the Bible, is not a God who creates the world and then lets it run its way, or a God who "idly observes from heaven what takes place on earth" (*Institutes* 1.16.4). "Indeed the principal purpose of Biblical history is to teach that the Lord watches over the ways of the saints with such great diligence that they do not even stumble over a stone" (*Institutes* 1.17.6). The providence of God sustains creation. In a sinful world, such a sustaining providence must take the form of unflagging determination to redeem creation, for without redemption we are lost to sin.

It is indeed the *whole* creation that God seeks to redeem. "We know that the whole creation has been groaning in labor pains until now," but God is at work "that the creation itself will be set free from its bondage to decay and will obtain the freedom of the glory of the children of God" (Rom. 8:22, 21). Human sin may have polluted God's good creation; much of the universe may seem to be moving along without purpose. But God's plan is not to "rescue" us (us Christians, us human beings) by pulling us out of a world that can then be abandoned to evil. In the providence of God, nothing is finally wasted or forgotten. Even the birds of the air and the flowers of the fields in all their beauty are included in the plan that God has for the redemption of creation.

> Do not fear, O soil;
> > be glad and rejoice,
> > for the Lord has done great things!
> Do not fear, you animals of the field,
> > for the pastures of the wilderness are green;
> the tree bears its fruit,
> > the fig tree and vine give their full yield.
> > > (Joel 2:21–22)

And if God cares for the soil and the animals of the field, how much more will God care for us, who are made in God's own image.

> Christ, when he declared that not even a tiny sparrow of little worth falls to the earth without the Father's will, immediately applies it in this way: that since we are of greater value than sparrows, we ought to realize that God watches over us with all the closer care; and he extends it so far that we may trust the hairs of our head are numbered. What else can we wish for ourselves if not even one hair can fall from our head without his will? (*Institutes* 1.17.6)

Even in human affairs, it is a great comfort to have confidence in the airplane pilot or the physician—to know that a competent and concerned expert is in charge. Though there may be dangers or rough passages ahead, the best that *could* be done *will* be done. But no human expert is infallible, and there can always be crises beyond any human control. It is only with God that we can trust that all things will for a certainty finally be brought to a good resolution.

God might have set about the work of sustaining and redeeming creation in many different ways. In fact, *the God of Abraham and Sarah chose a covenant people,* Israel, to be set apart as God's own people. It is a way of working that often makes us uncomfortable. If God is Lord of all creation, we want to say, then surely God is at work among all peoples. And indeed, no part of creation lies outside God's providence. Nevertheless, the Bible teaches us that this people is different: "Indeed, the whole earth is mine, but you shall be for me a priestly kingdom and a holy nation" (Ex. 19:5–6). Just as one creature is the creature made in the image of God, so one people is God's covenant people. Indeed, scripture makes quite astonishing claims. The great empires of the ancient Middle East rise and fall, and to the secular historian this small band of tribes called "Hebrews" or "Israel" might often nearly get lost in the shuffle. Yet the Bible claims that God brings Egypt's defeat for Israel's sake and that Babylon arises for the purpose of punishing Israel's sins. It might seem an impossibly egocentric way of looking at history, but the Bible proclaims its truth. God has chosen to manifest divine justice and mercy in a particular way in the particular history of this particular people, and Jesus Christ represents one climax of that particular history—the Word become flesh became Jewish flesh.

The Hebrew word *berith,* which we translate "covenant," can mean "contract" or "agreement" but also "promise," and that last translation may in this context be the most accurate. This is not a treaty between equals; Abraham has nothing that God needs in return. God simply chooses this people, and promises to remain faithful to that choice, come what may: "It was not because you were more numerous than any other people that the Lord set his heart on you and chose you. . . . It was because the Lord loved you and kept the oath that he swore to your ancestors" (Deut. 7:7–8). In due time God calls for a response: Hebrews are to be circumcised as a sign of the covenant, and eventually there is a code of laws. But all that comes later. First there is a call, and a promise: I will be your God and you will be my people.

It is the God of Abraham *and Sarah* who makes this promise. God promises Abraham to "make of you a great nation," (Gen. 12:2), but also says of Sarah, "I will bless her, and she shall give rise to nations" (Gen. 17:16). The promise is fulfilled from her womb. Israel was, like the other cultures of its time and place, a patriarchal society, but it was also a nation in which Sarah could receive God's blessing and promise and Deborah could be called to be judge and prophet.

The covenant is promised in God's *everlasting love*. "The gifts and the calling of God are irrevocable" (Rom. 11:29). We often fall into the habit of talking about "the Old Covenant" with Israel and "the New Covenant" in Christ, but the classic Reformed teaching was that we stand in the same covenant that was made with Abraham. The Westminster Confession identifies a "covenant of works" made with Adam and abrogated when Adam, "by his Fall . . . made himself incapable of life by that covenant" (6.039). Everything from there on is the covenant of grace, only "differently administered in the time of the law, and in the time of the gospel" (6.041). For a number of early Reformed theologians, even the rainbow and the promise to Noah, even God's making of garments for Adam and Eve as they are driven out of Eden, is already part of the covenant of grace. Abraham, without question, already lives under grace, the very model of the righteousness of faith.

The Old and New Testaments, then, represent different "administrations," or different "dispensations"—but one covenant. As Calvin explained:

> Whatever might be the amount of darkness under the law, the fathers were not ignorant of the road in which they ought to walk. Though the dawn is not equal to the splendor of noon, yet, as it is sufficient to direct a journey, travellers do not wait till the sun is fully risen. Their portion of light resembled the

dawn, which was enough to preserve them from all error, and guide them to everlasting blessedness.[1]

Christians have often been more willing to acknowledge sharing the covenant with Abraham and David than with their own Jewish neighbors. But the gifts and calling of God really are irrevocable. God made a promise to Israel, and God does not break promises. In Calvin's words, "He not only testified that he was, but also promised that he would ever be, their God" (*Institutes* 2.10.9).

The Christian gospel calls us to "make disciples of all nations" (Matt. 28:19). It would be a mistake, however, to draw too sharp a contrast between the "old dispensation," in which God's salvific plan concerned only one nation, and the new administration in Christ, in which salvation is for all nations. Israel's own self-understanding, after all, has always been that it is a servant people, called to be a light to the nations, *to bless all families of the earth.* God called Abraham so that "in you all the families of the earth shall be blessed" (Gen. 12:3). God works with this people in love and judgment and mercy, but the history of that work is available so that all people can see how God can work in the world. God has a plan for this people, but it is part of the plan that God has for all creation.

This is not something that it took Christians to discover; it was and is part of Israel's understanding of its covenant with God. The prophet Zechariah portrayed that understanding as dramatically as anyone when he foresaw the final day when "men from nations of every language shall take hold of a Jew, grasping his garment and saying, 'Let us go with you, for we have heard that God is with you' " (Zech. 8:23). Even as Israel rejoices that the signs of God's favor on this people show that God is at work in the world and keeps promises, yet at the same time its people acknowledge that this is a God who cares about all people, a God who brought Israel out of the land of Egypt but also "the Philistines from Caphtor and the Arameans from Kir" (Amos 9:7). Even the enemies of Israel are still encompassed by God's love. The great Rabbi Johanan told the story of how, after the Egyptian army was drowned in the sea at the Exodus, "the ministering angels wanted to sing a hymn at the destruction of the Egyptians, but God said: 'My children lie drowned in the sea, and you would sing?' "[2]

> A wandering Aramean was my ancestor; he went down into Egypt and lived there as an alien, few in number, and there he became a great nation, mighty and populous. When the Egyptians treated us harshly and afflicted us, by imposing hard labor on us, we cried to the Lord, the God of our ancestors; the Lord heard our voice and saw our affliction, our toil, and our oppression. The Lord brought us out of Egypt with a mighty hand and an outstretched arm, with a terrifying display of power, and with signs and wonders; and he brought us into this place and gave us this land, a land flowing with milk and honey. (Deut. 26:5–9)

This recital is central to Israel's faith; it defines the identity of the people and describes the character of their God. *Hearing their cry, God delivered the children of Israel from the house of bondage.* It is a story about having been aliens—oppressed, afflicted, and harshly treated—and about a God who hears the cries of the oppressed and rescues the afflicted from those who persecute them.

Israel's God kept reminding it of that history. The Ten Commandments themselves begin with a reminder: "I am the Lord your God, who brought you out of the land of Egypt, out of the house of slavery; you shall have no other gods before me" (Ex. 20:2–3). We think of that as a kind of preface, but Jews count it as the First Commandment, and there is something right about that: to remember, to know the identity of God through one's history, is already to be obedient to God's will.

The laws of Israel often include appeals to the memory of Egypt and the wilderness: "You shall not wrong or oppress a resident alien, for you were aliens in the land of Egypt. You shall not abuse any widow or orphan. If you do abuse them, when they cry out to me, I will surely heed their cry" (Ex. 22:21–23). These are not simply good moral injunctions; they follow from who this people is and who their God is. When the prophets condemn those who "oppress the poor" and "crush the needy" (Amos 4:1), they consciously speak to a people whose ancestors were slaves oppressed in the land of Egypt, who therefore ought to know better.

If we Christians share in this covenant, therefore, we claim that we are, by adoption, also the descendants of those who were in Egypt, who were aliens and oppressed. And our God is that same God who hears the cries of the downtrodden and the persecuted. And so the same lessons apply to us. If we are among those who oppress the poor, who "do not know" the despised minorities who live among us, then we stand under special condemnation, for, given our inheritance, we too ought to know better.

On the other hand, Christians who are among the downtrodden and the oppressed have recognized that the story of Israel in Egypt was in a special way their story, and Israel's God in a special way their God.

> When Israel was in Egypt's land, . . .
> Oppressed so hard they could not stand,
>> Let my people go!
> "No more shall they in bondage toil," . . .
> "Let them come out with Egypt's spoil,"
>> Let my people go!
> We need not always weep and moan,
> And wear these slavery chains forlorn.
>> Let my people go!
>
> Go down, Moses,
> way down in Egypt's land,
> Tell old Pharaoh,
>> Let my people go!

When African Americans have sung that song, their world has merged with the world of ancient Israel. They know that they too had been in Egypt and that their God is the God who heard the cry of those people, and who heard their cry. In the midst of a culture that has too often told African Americans and others that they were worthless and without dignity, this story provided the assurance that they were somebody—inheritors of a covenant with the Lord of all creation.

Most of us need to hear both messages. When we suffer affliction, we need the comfort of the story of the God who hears our cries. When we enjoy privilege and comfort that comes at the expense of others, when we ignore the downtrodden and the despised, we need to realize that we stand under the judgment of our covenantal heritage and the God of that covenant. Christian preaching, Reinhold Niebuhr used to say, ought to comfort the afflicted and afflict the comfortable.

The point of that "affliction," however, is not to load guilt on our shoulders. That rarely does much good for anybody. Instead, this side of our tradition can, for one thing, encourage those of us with wealth we could share or influence we could use to help people who need help. Beyond that, behind the appearance of comfort that wealth and power can provide, we are often afraid. What if I lose my job, or fail, or my life falls apart? If I have fallen into the trap of trying to guarantee the significance of my life by accumulating enough money or influence or fame, that can be a terrifying thought. The good news of a God who is singularly unimpressed with all those human signs of success can come to me too as liberation.

Loving us still, God made us heirs with Christ of the covenant. Jesus was a Jew who shared in the promises made to the descendants of Abraham. He fulfilled those promises, and he welcomes us as children of that covenant, "and if children, then heirs, heirs of God and joint heirs with Christ" (Rom. 8:17). We are like a wild olive branch grafted onto the rich root of the olive tree (Rom. 11:17). The 1987 General Assembly commended to the church for study a paper titled "A Theological Understanding of the Relationship Between Christians and Jews." This paper said (p. 9): "The church has not 'replaced' the Jewish people. Quite the contrary! The church, being made primarily of those who were once aliens and strangers to the covenants of promise, has been engrafted into the people of God."

"The Gospel," Calvin wrote, "did not so supplant the entire law as to bring forward a different way of salvation. Rather, it confirmed and satisfied whatever the law had promised, and gave substance to the shadows" (*Institutes* 2.9.4). After all, Christ proclaimed, "Do not think that I have come to abolish the law or the prophets; I have come not to abolish but to fulfill" (Matt. 5:17).

Our Jewish partners in conversation will be justifiably suspicious if we try to claim that there are no differences in belief between us. We believe we know good news that they do not accept. We believe that in Jesus, God's promises to Israel have been fulfilled; they do not. We should be honest about where we disagree. But we should not speak to them as past covenant partners who have been superseded, but rather as descendants of Abraham to whom God made an irrevocable promise.

God remains always faithful. God does not abandon us, even in our sin; God remains faithful, even when we are faithless. God does not even simply stand waiting for us to make the first move. *Like a mother who will not forsake her nursing child, like a father who runs to welcome the prodigal home,* God is always comforting us; God is rushing toward us in grace long before we have returned home.

Luke 15 tells the story of the "prodigal son." The younger son asks for his inheritance in advance, leaves home, and squanders his property "in dissolute living" (wastefulness is what the word "prodigal" means). Destitute, he is reduced to caring for pigs as a hired servant, hungry, wishing he could even eat the food given the pigs. So he decides to swallow his pride, face his medicine, and return home. "But while he was still far off, his father saw him and was filled with compassion; he ran and put his arms around him and kissed him" (v. 20).

It is a story that reminds us of God's mercy, and Christians have used the image of God as "father" to try to convey that loving forgiveness. Line 28 raised some questions about how to use that term in contemporary context; these lines open up some other possibilities.

First, in preaching and pastoral care we should remember that some human parents lack these divine attributes. Some Christians had abusive or uncaring parents, or grew up without parents. To some, we need to say, not, "Remember your mother and father—well, God is like that," but instead, "Try to put aside the hurt and the pain of your memories, and trust that, whatever your experience of human parents, there is One who loves and cares and never abandons." That is the context of the passage in Isaiah to which line 49 alludes: "Even these may forget, yet I will not forget you" (Isa. 49:15).

Second, we need to remember the *kind* of father being described. Jesus' own references to his "Abba" at once preserved
and challenged many of the usual connotations of "Father,"
particularly in traditional cultures: for this "Abba" is not a stern,
commanding patriarch but a gentle, sharing "Daddy." (See line
28.) The typical father of an ancient Middle Eastern village
would never *run*—that would mean lifting up his robe and looking totally undignified. Where our salvation is concerned, however, the loving God of the Bible does not rest on dignity.

Third, and finally, it is worth remembering that scripture
does not compare God only to a father.

> Can a woman forget her nursing child,
>> or show no compassion for the child of her womb?

God asks Isaiah.

> Even these may forget,
>> yet I will not forget you.
>>> (Isa. 49:15)

Indeed:

> As a mother comforts her child,
>> so I will comfort you.
>>> (Isa. 66:13)

God, Jesus says, is not only like a shepherd who will seek the
one lost sheep when ninety-nine are already in the fold, but
also like a woman with ten silver coins who loses one of them
and will search the house until she finds it (Luke 15:8).

Even amid predominantly "Father" language, scripture
sometimes talks about the "womb" of God, from which God
has given birth:

> "Has the rain a father
>> or who has begotten the drops of dew?
> From whose womb did the ice come from forth,
>> and who has given birth to the hoarfrost of heaven?"
>>> (Job 38:28–29)

If God gives birth to creation, so also Israel can come from
God's womb:

> Listen to me, O house of Jacob,
>> all the remnant of the house of Israel,
> who have been borne by me from your birth,
>> carried from the womb;
> even to your old age I am he,
>> even when you turn gray I will carry you.
> I have made, and I will bear;
>> I will carry and will save.
>
> (Isa. 46:3–4)

Even more daringly, the prophet imagines God crying out like a woman in labor:

> For a long time I have held my peace,
>> I have kept still and restrained myself;
> now I will cry out like a woman in labor,
>> I will gasp and pant.
>
> (Isa. 42:14)

These biblical images challenge our preconceptions. Here is this God the text refers to as "he" who gives birth from "his" womb and gasps and pants like a woman in labor. God is very personal, no "it," but keeps breaking out of all the human categories we might want to use.

It is helpful, then, to think of God as "like a mother" as well as "like a father." Such a strategy enriches rather than reduces our language about God. We continue to call God "Father." Quite apart from other considerations, it is dangerous to imply that nurturing, loving-kindness, and accessibility are somehow only "maternal," "feminine" characteristics. Mothers can be tough too; fathers can be gentle too. It would be wrong to separate these two lines in the text of the statement as if they pointed to different characteristics of God. The father in the story of the prodigal son is a good example, therefore—a father who eagerly, emotionally (like a mother! our cultural stereotypes invite us to say) runs out to forgive his son.

Interestingly enough, that story captures the dominant theme of Old Testament references to God as Father. The Old Testament explicitly calls God "Father" only twelve times. Five of them point to a special relationship between God and the king of Israel. In each of the other seven, God the Father is recalling children home, seeking reconciliation with them.³ When we see God as like a mother *or* as like a father, if we stand in the biblical tradition, what we do most of all is to point to God's love and forgiveness and faithfulness.

God is faithful still. The human journey begins with God, for God is our creator, and it ends with God, for God is our destination and our hope and our home. When we journey in the land of sin, we are lost, we have gone astray. When we do find a path home it is not because we were clever enough to find our own way or brave enough to battle through the wilderness on our own, but because the God who is always waiting for us comes out in love to seek us and to rescue us. Our sin is not without cost. We really do get lost, and our wanderings and the suffering we endure in their midst are real. And we see in the cross the cost of our sins to God. But the real cost gets paid, and before we have even tried to complete our journey we encounter God running toward us. "What if some were unfaithful? Will their faithlessness nullify the faithfulness of God? By no means!" (Rom. 3:3–4).

> For his anger is but for a moment;
> his favor is for a lifetime.
>
> (Ps. 30:5)

And longer than just a lifetime. Each of the three middle sections of this Statement concludes on a note of hope, a hope that reaches beyond even the end of this life. "God raised this Jesus from the dead, . . . delivering us from death to life eternal" (lines 23, 26). "God is faithful still" (line 51). "We watch for God's new heaven and new earth, praying, 'Come, Lord Jesus!' " (lines 75–76). All three conclusions therefore both recall the opening and anticipate the conclusion of the whole Statement. It is in life *and in death* that we belong to God. And nothing in life or death can separate us from the love of God in Christ Jesus our Lord.

Trust in God the Holy Spirit

10. The Life of the Spirit
(Lines 52–57)

52   We trust in God the Holy Spirit,
53   everywhere the giver and renewer of life.
54   The Spirit justifies us by grace through faith,
55   sets us free to accept ourselves and to love God and
           neighbor,
56   and binds us together with all believers
57   in the one body of Christ, the Church.

Lines 52–76 discuss what Karl Barth called "the third form of faith in the one God."[1] This third form of the faith, faith in the Holy Spirit, is implied in the other two forms, just as they are implied in this form. That is what it means to declare that in trusting in the one triune God (line 5) *we trust in God the Holy Spirit.*

The Christian faith in all its parts and direction is "doxological"—that is, it is a form of praise—because faith is a response to the Subject who is praiseworthy. Christian faith in all its forms involves not just knowing *about* God but trusting *in* God. It is by the Holy Spirit in particular, though, that what we know about God's redemptive and creative activity comes alive as adoring, committed, *ethically vital trust* in God.

Few have written as well about this as the great American colonial theologian Jonathan Edwards, in his treatment of the "religious affections" that are due to the "powerful, quickening, saving influences" of the Spirit.[2] Edwards held together understanding and affection as few theologians succeed in doing:

As there is no true religion where there is nothing else but affection, so there is no true religion where there is no religious affection. As on the one hand, there must be light in the understanding, as well as an affected fervent heart; where there is heat without light, there can be nothing divine or heavenly in that heart; so on the other hand, where there is a kind of light without heat, a head stored with notions and speculations, with a cold and unaffected heart, there can be nothing divine in that light, that knowledge is no true spiritual knowledge of divine things. If the great things of religion are rightly understood, they will affect the heart.[3]

The Holy Spirit is more than the power *by* whom we come to worship and obey God. The Holy Spirit is God, and as such is also the one *on* whom we call, the one whose freedom to be for us and the rest of creation is the presupposition of creaturely life and freedom. We experience the Holy Spirit as gift. Whatever else is said about the grace of God as God's love and empowerment must be understood as descriptive of the Holy Spirit, upon whom we are dependent and in whose steadfastness we participate in life and in the renewal of life. "In all she does the Church lives by the Holy Spirit and invokes his powerful aid. Through him she consecrates all mankind and the whole creation, that the world may become an offering, to the praise of its Creator and Saviour."[4]

Lines 52–57 deal with the reality and benefits of the Holy Spirit. God the Holy Spirit is the giver and renewer of life *everywhere* (lines 52–53)—we begin with that affirmation. Believers make this confession about the Spirit's *universal* presence, however, primarily because of the *particular* freedom they experience in their new life together as members of the body of Christ; and so we will turn to that topic in lines 54–57.

We trust in God the Holy Spirit, everywhere the giver and renewer of life (lines 52–53). This claim cuts in both directions. It says that wherever there is life, that life is due to the presence and activity of the Holy Spirit. It also says that what life is, whatever quality (not just quantity) of existence constitutes life, needs to be understood as the good gift of the Holy Spirit.

That life is fundamentally good is a confession of faith based on the goodness of God, without whom we would not be, whose love quickens and orders the love among us creatures.

One of the central paradoxes of the Christian faith is that it is only by the *special* presence of the Holy Spirit that the church is enabled to witness to the *universal* presence and work of the Holy Spirit. It is the church that knows whom it calls upon when it prays,

> Come, Holy Spirit,
> We sure do need you now—Mmmmm.[5]

It is the church that knows an experience of rebirth which it recognizes as the work of the Holy Spirit. Part of the experience of rebirth, however, is the joyous recognition that the whole of creation belongs to God, and that the Holy Spirit is not confined either to one's own personal experience or to the boundaries of the church.

One of the strongest ways of confessing the divinity of the Holy Spirit is to address the Holy Spirit with praise and petition. At the Council of Nicaea of 325, the eternal Word become flesh as Jesus Christ was confessed to be "of the same being [*homoousios*] with the Father." Parallel to this confession of the divinity of the eternal Son was the confession of the divinity of the eternal Spirit. The Council of Constantinople in 381 reworked the Nicene Creed into roughly the form in which we recite it today, expanding the section on the Holy Spirit to declare, "We believe in the Holy Spirit, the Lord, the giver of life, who proceeds from the Father, who with the Father and the Son is worshiped and glorified, who spoke through the prophets." For complicated reasons, Western, Latin-speaking Christians gradually came to say that the Holy Spirit proceeds "from the Father *and the Son*," a difference that remains a significant source of disagreement with Eastern Orthodox churches. For our purposes here, however, the main point is simply that the church affirmed the Holy Spirit as fully God—not something made (the force of "proceeds" is to contrast with "was created"), not part of creation, but one of the Persons of the triune God, and therefore worthy of worship.

Those things for which the Holy Spirit is worshiped, adored, and invoked are universal in scope. That is, it belongs to the very nature of Christian worship and discipleship to discern and rejoice in and make common cause with the continually new work of the Holy Spirit *wherever* life and healing and discovery and invention and authentic expression occur in creation, including the whole human community. After all, the Holy Spirit is God, the One in whom we live and move and have our being. The special gifts to the church and to believers are not places where the Holy Spirit, previously absent, begins to be present. They are applications to the church and to persons of the deployment, the economy, of the Spirit, who is everywhere present and active where life is given and renewed. We are permitted to speak about the Holy Spirit's being in us, active in our lives, powerfully experienced by believers only insofar as our intention thereby is that we experience a new dimension of what it means to be caught up into, to realize the extent of, the special presence and activity of the same Spirit who is universally the giver and provider and renewer of life.

If we consider the Spirit's work as regenerator apart from the Spirit's work as creator, we lose sight of the magnitude and concreteness of the new life—and we lose sight of whose we are even before we come to recognize whose we are. Our belief does not cause us to belong to God. The great medieval hymn "Veni, Creator Spiritus" expresses this beautifully:

> Veni, Creator Spiritus,
> Mentes tuorum visita:
> Imple superna gratia
> Quae tu creasti pectora.

The usual English translation runs: "Come, Holy Spirit,/From thy bright heavenly throne!/Come, take possession of our souls,/And make them all thine own." This has the advantage of rhyming "throne" and "own," but it completely misses the point that the Holy Spirit is being invoked to come upon and to fill those things which the Holy Spirit, being their Creator, already possesses: "Come, Creator Spirit. Visit the minds of those who are yours. Fill with extraordinary grace those hearts which you created."

The Spirit justifies us by grace through faith, sets us free to accept ourselves and to love God and neighbor, and binds us together with all believers in the one body of Christ, the Church (lines 54–56). Syntactically, this is one of the most difficult sentences in the Brief Statement of Faith. The difficulty grows out of trying to point to different ways of expressing the same reality—the gracious character of the new life that freely forgiven sinners have together in Christ—without suggesting a misleading sequence in the Christian life. Though one of the most difficult sentences, it is also one of the most important to get right, since it summarizes the dynamics of the freedom of the life together in Christ enabled by the Holy Spirit.

The Heidelberg Catechism is of great help in getting the meaning straight, especially because of the way it holds together four things in the sequence of Questions 53–56, which follows the sequence of the Apostles' Creed.

> Q. 53. **What do you believe concerning "the Holy Spirit"?** A. First, that, with the Father and the Son, he is equally eternal God; second, that God's Spirit is also given to me, preparing me through a true faith to share in Christ and all his benefits, that he comforts me and will abide with me forever.

> Q. 54. **What do you believe concerning "the Holy Catholic Church"?** A. I believe that, from the beginning to the end of the world, and from among the whole human race, the Son of God, by his Spirit and his Word, gathers, protects, and preserves for himself, in the unity of the true faith, a congregation chosen for eternal life. Moreover, I believe that I am and forever will remain a living member of it.

> Q. 55. **What do you understand by "the communion of saints"?** A. First, that believers one and all, as partakers of the Lord Christ, and all his treasures and gifts, share in one fellowship. Second, that each one ought to know that he is obliged to use his gifts freely and with joy for the benefit and welfare of other members.

Q. 56. What do you believe concerning "the forgiveness of sins"? A. That for the sake of Christ's reconciling work, God will no more remember my sins or the sinfulness with which I have to struggle all my life long; but that he graciously imparts to me the righteousness of Christ so that I may never come into condemnation. (4.053–4.056)

The Spirit justifies us by grace through faith in the sense that the Spirit unites us to Christ and so makes us sharers in Christ's righteousness.

The Holy Spirit reveals to believers the fuller implications of the things that are Christ's—what contemporary theologian Jan Lochman calls the contemporizing office of the Holy Spirit. This is the office most fully described in John's Gospel, chapters 14–16. It involves more than providing disciples with a fuller memory and a deeper understanding of who Christ is and what is the nature of his saving work. The Holy Spirit is poured out into our hearts in such a way that we are made participants in Christ and Christ's benefits. Or, to put it differently, by receiving the promised gift of the Holy Spirit the disciples are made active participants in the presence of the end times ushered in by the life and death and resurrection of Jesus the Christ. Their new life is the life of the end times, whose content is their comembership in the body of Christ.

To use Calvin's term, the Holy Spirit is the "bond" that unites us to Christ and to one another in him, so that whatever is his is applied to us.[6] That is what it means to say that his righteousness is reckoned or "imputed" to us, not because of anything we bring to that relationship—including "our" faith, lest we treat our faith as something that merits God's favor! For no other reason (as if that were not enough!) than God's love, the estrangement of sin has been overcome so that whoever is in Christ is a new creature (2 Cor. 5). Or, to use a different image, since we have been baptized into Christ's death we are made sharers in his resurrection: "We have been buried with him by baptism into death, so that, just as Christ was raised from the dead by the glory of the Father, so we too might walk in newness of life" (Rom. 6:4).

The prominence given in the Statement to justification by grace though faith serves to emphasize that whatever else is said in the rest of the Brief Statement of Faith about the church's equipment, the church's mission, and the church's hope, these are simply another way of stating the unmerited mercy of God, which sets believers free for walking in newness of life. The Barmen Declaration accurately summarizes the Reformed tradition's emphasis on the freedom of the gospel as "freedom from" which is simultaneously "freedom for"—we are freed from sin and death so that we might walk in newness of life:

> As Jesus Christ is God's assurance of the forgiveness of all our sins, so in the same way and with the same seriousness he is also God's mighty claim upon our whole life. Through him befalls us a joyful deliverance from the godless fetters of this world for a free, grateful service to his creatures. We reject the false doctrine, as though there were areas of our life in which we would not belong to Jesus Christ, but to other lords—areas in which we would not need justification and sanctification through him. (8.14–8.15)

The new relationship of living as forgiven sinners enabled by the Holy Spirit to grow in life together in Christ—that is precisely what it means to be "justified" (made righteous) and set in the way of sanctification (the growth in that new life). There simply is no other content to justification than this righteousness of Christ, which is really and freely made ours by the Holy Spirit's uniting us together in him. And, we can be sure, "justification" is not some process we go through propelled by some fuel called "grace" until we achieve the goal of being united to Christ! Grace is precisely the favor of God and the empowering Holy Spirit, who moves us to take the gospel to heart, so that we repent and include ourselves among those who are forgiven and thereby enabled to live out the daily conversion which is newness of life.

The forgiveness and newness of life that are freely given are for persons, for each of us, in the most concrete circumstances of life—as it is, in all the complexity of this world. It means that we, really forgiven and restored sinners, are also active subjects responding with new lives. Our response is by the power of the Spirit—and it is therefore really *our* response, and not just God's response to God. Where the Spirit is, there is freedom, according to Second Corinthians—freedom for humans to be transformed into the likeness of Christ's image: "Now the Lord is the Spirit, and where the Spirit of the Lord is, there is freedom. And all of us, with unveiled faces, seeing the glory of the Lord as though reflected in a mirror, are being transformed into the same image from one degree of glory to another; for this comes from the Lord, the Spirit" (2 Cor. 3:17–18). It is a mark of the Holy Spirit's presence that humans are freed to respond and to share in God's own ongoing work for the whole of creation. To say the Holy Spirit permits us to experience the power of the Spirit does not mean that the Spirit overwhelms and forces us. Rather, as Karl Barth put it, the Holy Spirit is experienced as one "who sets us on our feet as partners. The Holy Spirit wants us to stand up and walk on our own legs as the Spirit's partners. In other words, the Spirit wants *us* to believe, to love, to hope."[7]

This new life is not arbitrary or whimsical, as if God were mocking God's people in giving them the commandments. On the contrary, life in the Spirit is freedom to practice being guided by the law, which gives hope and structure to Christian freedom. It is to this, the third use of the law (positive guidance in living the Christian life; see commentary on line 34), that line 55 alludes. It is the summary of the Ten Commandments, with, however, a curious variation which is as risky as it is timely. As freely forgiven sinners joined to Christ and one another by the Holy Spirit, we are set *free to accept ourselves and to love God and neighbor.* This could be heard as slipping in a certain trendiness, which actually goes so far as to make self-acceptance the root change of which the rest of the things in this section are variations. There is, however, something far different going on in this line, that is, the lifting up and making explicit of what is already implied in Jesus' summary of the law. That summary enjoins us to "love the Lord your God with all your heart, and with all your soul, and with all your mind, and with all your strength" and "love your neighbor as yourself" (Mark 12:30–31).

The "as yourself" is more than an appeal based on egoism. It implies treating another person as the subject of love, a love that one already knows something about from valuing oneself as belonging to the people whom God calls into being by the covenant. That covenantal people know God to be the God who has created and redeemed us. Accepting ourselves as forgiven and as a part of the goodness of God's creation is part of what it means to love God and neighbor, and is indeed part of the reciprocity of love. There is no genuine love of God or of neighbor that does not also bring with it the knowledge that the gospel also applies to oneself. According to Esther de Waal (who is writing here most immediately about the monastic life):

> It is just because we are accepted by Christ that we can accept others and accept ourselves. Self-love is important, fundamentally important. The novice begins with the process of stripping himself [herself] or letting himself [herself] be stripped of the empirical self, so that the real self may emerge in the common life of the community, which is the school of love. In this school of love three dimensions of love grow together: love of self, love of the brethren [sisters], love of God. To know myself without any complacency and without any self-justification means really loving myself, knowing myself as I really am, set free from wishful thinking. Only after that honesty, standing naked before the God who loves, accepts and does not judge, can I turn and present that same image, stripped of all false colors, to all the other people in my life. . . . The practice of obedience [she is speaking of the Benedictine Rule] means that I lay aside idols, and empty myself at my center, so that I can reach out to others. And above all, openness to growth means that I bring some dynamic quality of love into relationships, so that I am ready to change, to renew the pattern of marriage, to encourage my children to grow into freedom, to work at a friendship to prevent it from fossilizing at some past stage of my life.[8]

The Spirit *binds us together with all believers in the one body of Christ, the Church* (lines 56–57). Being bound together by the Spirit into the body of Christ is the foundation of the Christian life, not its culmination. Of the many images that Christians use for the church, the image of the body most emphasizes the interconnectedness and reciprocal responsibility of those who are joined to Christ and to one another by the Spirit. An arm, a foot, a head cannot survive without the rest of the body; indeed, they are what they are precisely as parts of an interconnected body.

One of the central paradoxes of the Christian faith is the fact that believers discover their *freedom* in living the *discipline* of comembership in the body of Christ. Christian freedom is being bound to one another in a common life, just as the freedom of ministering is being bound to serve the Word. Those are not, however, different freedoms, for the freedom of life together as *believers* is the common response of faith occasioned by the common hearing of the Word in its several forms. That is where faith comes from, hearing the Word, and that is how faith is confirmed, corrected, strengthened. God accommodates to our condition through the ordinary means of grace, through the historically conditioned forms of the Word—proclamation, sacraments, discipline of the community, prayer. These are effective not by some quality inherent in these acts themselves, but by the power of the Holy Spirit, who moves us to take the gospel, mediated in these various forms, to heart.

Therefore, we turn to the next lines of the Brief Statement of Faith (lines 58–64), devoted to the ordinary means by which God equips the church. We are not turning to some completely new topic, but precisely to the ways by which all believers are bound together in the one body of Christ, the church. The section after that (lines 65–71), which deals with the church's mission, is also closely connected with the starting point of the discussion of the Spirit. The inclusiveness and quality of believers' life together is integral to the church's being an effective sign of what God wills for the whole of creation. To say that we are bound by the Spirit to all believers is to covenant again and again that none be excluded from—or marginalized within—that community whose life together is a form of witnessing.

11. The Gathering of the Church
(Lines 58–64)

58   The same Spirit
59   who inspired the prophets and apostles
60   rules our faith and life in Christ through Scripture,
61   engages us through the Word proclaimed,
62   claims us in the waters of baptism,
63   feeds us with the bread of life and the cup of salvation,
64   and calls women and men to all ministries of the Church.

These lines form one sentence identifying the subject *(The same Spirit who inspired the prophets and apostles)*, whose dynamic effect on the community is proclaimed with a cascade of active verbs *(rules . . . engages . . . claims . . . feeds . . . and calls)*.

Each of these verbs deals with one of the ways the community is gathered and sent, corrected and enlivened, ordered and freed. They deal with what Calvin calls the helps by which we are invited into the society of Christ and sustained in it. They are various forms of the Word by which God accommodates to our condition, moving men and women to hear and take to heart the gospel and to live a common life ordered by it through the gifts given for the calling, upbuilding, and sending of the community of believers. The "communion of the Holy Spirit" as experienced in this life is a mediated fellowship; it is a historically transmitted and conditioned reality in which we share through the right use of these gifts of God for the people of God.

The same Spirit who inspired the prophets and apostles . . . This phrase makes a connection between inspiration and what follows,

in the next line, about scripture. It makes that connection in
such a way, however, that the focus is on the steadfastness, the
continuous identity, of the Spirit. The focus is on the fact that
the Spirit who rules our faith and life in Christ through scripture
today and in the future is the very same Spirit by whose power
the Word of the Lord came to the people of the Old Testament
and those of the New Testament. There is in this line a reso-
nance with the Nicene Creed's affirmation that we believe in the
Holy Spirit, the Lord and giver of life, "who spoke by the
prophets." That provision was important then, in the fourth century, as it is now and for the same reason. It takes a stand against
those who would treat the Christian faith as intelligible and
meaningful apart from God's gracious presence and activity, already known among the people of the Old Testament. In claiming that "the Bible" (in the singular) is made up of the Old
Testament and the New Testament—prophets as well as apostles—the church is making the fundamental claim that *the same
God* is witnessed to, and graciously experienced, in each part.
This is so no matter how differently, manifestly, more powerfully
that same reality was experienced, the church claims, after the
coming of the Messiah.

Far from detracting from the authority of scripture by not at-
tempting to restate some view of verbal inspiration, these lines
set forth what is really an audacious and strikingly exalted view
of the authority of scripture. Obviously the very term "authority" today has many negative connotations. To some people it
suggests nothing more than imposed sanctions which override a
person's consent. Yet "authority" also means a power that
moves us willingly, that catches us up so that we sense our own
place and share in the reality to which an event or a story or a
teaching refers. In the context of what immediately precedes it
(The same Spirit who inspired the prophets and apostles) and what
immediately follows it *(engages us through the Word proclaimed)*, line 60 is a powerful assertion of this second kind of
authority. It is *the Spirit who rules our faith and life in Christ
through Scripture*. The correct relation between the Spirit and
the written form of the Word is preserved here. We are not
hereby permitted to be ruled by anything we may conveniently
choose to call "the Spirit," be that a whim or a firm conviction

or a popular movement or a favored tradition or a collection of best intentions. It is *through scripture* that the Spirit rules, and that which is ruled in this way is our faith and life in Christ. There are other things in which the Spirit does not rule the same way. That means, for example, that the scriptures are not to be confused with a civil code or with a guide to scientific cosmology or with a reliable medical handbook or with any of the other ways through which, so the church confesses, the Holy Spirit, who is also *Creator Spiritus*—the creating Spirit *everywhere the giver and renewer of life*—works. "The Spirit blows where it chooses," and works in many ways, but the way the Spirit works through scripture is special, and it is in this special way that the Spirit *rules our faith and life* as Christians.

Obviously there is considerable overlap between the lessons of scripture and all sorts of worldly wisdom and common sense, as believers seek to live out the gospel's relevance in every area of life; but when it comes to identifying and correcting and ordering our faith and life in Christ—that which is diversely practiced in whatever area of life we find ourselves set—it is through scripture that the Spirit rules. In this sense, line 60 is carrying forward the implications of the first of the Barmen Declaration's "evangelical truths": "Jesus Christ, as he is attested for us in Holy Scripture, is the one Word of God which we have to hear and which we have to trust and obey in life and in death" (8.11). The first sentence on the Bible in the Confession of 1967 echoes Barmen here: "The one sufficient revelation of God is Jesus Christ, the Word of God incarnate, to whom the Holy Spirit bears unique and authoritative witness through the Holy Scriptures, which are received and obeyed as the word of God written. The Scriptures are not a witness among others, but the witness without parallel" (9.27).

"Rules our faith and life in Christ through Scripture . . ." is at the head of the other activities of the Spirit that follow in this section. That says that ruling our faith and life through scripture is not simply one thing alongside other activities of the Spirit. Rather, those other activities are ways that ruling through scripture takes place, and apart from which one would be left with a static and isolated view of the scriptures.

The Word proclaimed, through which the Spirit engages us, is preaching that is out of scripture and that takes seriously the need to interpret scripture. In this way, it becomes again and again not just the written form of the Word of God to someone else and to some other culture but ours, addressed to our condition, to this time and place. Once again: It is the Spirit who is the Subject, the one who *engages us through the Word proclaimed.* By the power of the Spirit, when one preaches out of and interprets the written form of the Word, what happens—what "befalls us," what becomes an event—is nothing less than another form of the Word of God. The Second Helvetic Confession puts it sharply: "Preaching of the Word of God is the Word of God!" (5.004). In the Reformed tradition, at least, there is a certain order to the way the church is ruled by the Spirit through scripture. Preaching the Word is *not* just preaching, and not just preaching something else which can be illustrated from scriptures, treated as a convenient repository of useful symbols. Preaching the Word is given preeminence in the continual reform of the church, and indeed is that primary form of proclamation which theology exists to serve.

Of course, with so much weight given to the role of preaching the Word in equipping and correcting the church, all the greater the peril if it be neglected or corrupted or taken off into the Babylonian captivity of pulpit oratory. The Spirit *engages us through the Word proclaimed.* That may entail a whole range of things which also are good by-products, as it were, of being engaged by the Word proclaimed. But to be "engaged through the Word proclaimed" has a very concrete meaning. It means so to encounter the presence of the new reign of God in Christ's presence that we are moved to repent and believe the good news. It means not just assenting to the truth about this or that reality, even the reality that the righteous God is merciful to others. It means embracing, holding onto with converting delight, the truth of the gospel as applying also to oneself. That engagement occurs over and over and over again in response to the Word. It is every day a matter of the way the gospel moves us to the conviction of sin and the assurance of pardon and the empowerment to walk in newness of life. It is that newness of life which is faith active in the loving care of others, and faith active in accepting others' loving care of self. This newness of life is living out the realization of one's co-belonging to God in a community that is a sign of the justice, freedom, and peace God wills for the whole of creation.

Lines 62 and 63, *claims us in the waters of baptism, feeds us with the bread of life and the cup of salvation*, refer to the sacraments. Technically the sacraments are, along with preaching, also forms of "proclamation" of the Word. Even when "proclamation" is used synonymously with "preaching," the sacraments of Baptism and the Lord's Supper are understood (following Augustine's definition) to be visible forms of the Word.[1]

That traditional definition of a sacrament—a visible form of the Word—may well be inadequate to convey, today, the reality to which it originally referred. Put negatively, the sacraments are *not* "illustrations" or "visual aids" which make more vivid what was "talked about" in preaching! Preaching is not "talking about" a Subject who is absent, but what happens when the Subject *graciously* takes human words and *really* makes the gospel the content of what is spoken. On the one hand, there is nothing automatic about the relation between what the preacher does, or does not do, and the gospel's taking root in the heart. There is nothing inherent in the act of preaching itself, no quasi-magical quality to it, that guarantees an accurate and powerful witness and reception. On the other hand, *because Christ is true to his promises*, because we know, with the full assurance of faith, that God really accommodates to our condition, we can trust that the human words of the preacher are made to be vehicle of God's very address to us.

In the same way, the sacraments are not memoranda about an absent Subject or about a foggily distant event. They are, by grace, effective signs of grace, and there are the same two dangers to beware of with regard to the sacraments that we noted regarding preaching. There is the danger of superstition. That is the danger of treating the sacraments almost magically by confusing the signs (the elements of water and of bread and wine, and the actions done with them) with the reality they are intended to proclaim and offer. And there is the opposite danger, that of spiritualizing the sacraments. That is the danger of rendering them superfluous by almost completely separating the signs from what is signified, and therefore saying that the signs themselves have no importance. Calvin deplored such "spiritualizing" because it refused to take seriously the promises of Christ to use earthly means for our participation in the reality of the new life in him. Calvin is clear that when speaking of the sacraments we are to use the terms "spiritual" and "spiritually" only because it is by the power of the Holy *Spirit* that the signs are joined to the reality, which is Christ clothed with his benefits.

There are two main reasons given in Reformed confessions for celebrating the sacraments, namely, to strengthen the faith of believers and to bear public witness. The word frequently used for the first reason is that the sacraments "confirm" faith, which is a richer term than strengthen, though it includes it. The faith of the community is reidentified, is rearticulated, is corrected and focused back again on what is essential, is livened up and made strong. The second reason cannot be separated from the first. The faith being confirmed is by its nature a witnessing trust. Faith does not focus on itself any more than the church focuses on itself. The celebration of the sacraments is, of course, for believers' mutual comfort and correction; but that celebration is also part of the cost of discipleship in a world where the community's ultimate loyalties bring it into conflict with other loyalties. The presence in the world of a community whose ultimate loyalties and trust are focused on God's benevolence for the whole of creation is itself a witness to a reality beyond the world. The perseverance of such a community of faith, visibly evident also when it celebrates the sacraments, is itself an effective sign of the goodness—the justice, freedom, and peace—which God wills for all.

The Holy Spirit *claims us* in baptism. The Brief Statement of Faith sets forth no single understanding of baptism, nor does it enter the debate over infant baptism and believer's baptism. It seeks to identify the heart of the matter—the conviction that we are claimed in the waters of baptism. This reinforces the guiding conviction that runs throughout the document: *In life and in death we belong to God.* Instead of being alienated from God, and instead of being strangers and aliens to the promises, we are adopted, brought into, made part of the household of

God, freed to participate in life together in Christ. We are brought into the household of God as we are made to share in the life, death, and resurrection of Christ. This means repentance, forgiveness of sins, and being empowered to share in Christ's own continuing ministry.

It is important to bear in mind the twin dangers regarding sacraments mentioned above. On the one hand, the act of baptism is not to be neglected on the ground that it is a "mere symbol." For one thing, such a view misunderstands the nature of symbol. There is no such thing as a "mere" symbol. By definition, a symbol points beyond itself to a reality in which it shares.[2] In this case the reality is the new life in Christ, which entails repentance and new birth, forgiveness of sins, deliverance from alien lords, life as people anointed with the Spirit, freedom to serve God and the world which is the object of God's love. The waters used in baptism should be far more congruent with the magnitude of this reality than the paltry finger-dipping and slightly humidifying practice (or malpractice) that still is too apparent in many of our congregations.

On the other hand, the act of baptism is not to be considered as the occasion when we begin to belong to God, or an act that must be done before we begin to share in the new life in Christ. That is what the Reformed confessions were insisting on when they called the sacrament of baptism "a sign of the covenant,"[3] meaning by that the covenant of grace which obtained for all God's people in the Old and New Testaments. In the Old Testament the sign was different—it was circumcision that set apart God's people—and the reality was experienced differently, but the covenantal reality was the same as in the New Testament. The Spirit moves people to hear the Word accurately and powerfully; the Spirit moves us to repent and to accept the forgiveness of sins and the mission to which we are called as forgiven sinners. The outward sign of this fundamental reality is the act of baptism, in which the congregation of believers gathers to welcome others as Christ has welcomed them, to acknowledge their place among the people of God and renew their part in the covenant.

It is an act by which the reality is acknowledged, and applied not just to the persons being baptized. It is an act in which those who have already been baptized renew their commitment to live as comembers of the body of Christ. Baptism is not an isolated act, some sort of necessary transaction, some cleansing ritual necessary to avoid hell. That was the reasoning and fear behind emergency baptisms. Baptism is part of a continual process of death to the old self and rebirth of the new—of growth in grace, of edification in the faith throughout various stages of development and seasons of life—all of which occurs within the matrix of the community of faith. Somewhere, sometime, that process includes a specific moment of witting, critical, public confession of faith on the part of each member of the believing community. That moment occurs at a different stage of the process in the case of believer's baptism and infant baptism. But that moment, in either case, is not to be separated from the ongoing reconfessing and growth that occur within the loving, admonishing, encouraging, witnessing fellowship of forgiven sinners. That is why "private baptisms" are almost a contradiction in terms, and why various ways of renewing baptismal vows (not being "rebaptized") are important for continuing renewal of the congregation's sense of its fundamental identity.

In the Lord's Supper the Holy Spirit *feeds us with the bread of life and the cup of salvation.* We are claimed and made members of God's household, and we are nourished in the new life with the lavish banquet set before us. This is not just an actual eating and drinking, although it is certainly that; it is, rather, feeding on Christ by faith, by which our union with him and sharing in his benefits are enjoyed ever again. The statement uses strong language to refer to the reality being celebrated in the Lord's Supper—the language of participation (or communion, fellowship, sharing) taken from 1 Corinthians 10:16: "The cup of blessing that we bless, is it not a sharing in the blood of Christ? The bread that we break, is it not a sharing in the body of Christ?" In its doctrine of the Lord's Supper, the Reformed tradition—reflecting in this point a much broader history of interpretation—has read this with John 6 in mind, where Christ is identified as "the bread of life." Christ does not begin to be the bread of life for us when we celebrate the Lord's

Supper, but we actively participate in a reality that is already present and freely offered as we receive with faith the signs through which Christ accommodates to our condition.

Here is the same seriousness we noted earlier about the signs—both the appointed elements and the actions with them—and the same sobriety about not confusing them with the reality they serve. With that necessary caution in place, however, there is a boldness with which we are bidden to accept what is lavishly bestowed upon us through the Lord's Supper. By the power of the Holy Spirit, we grow more and more into the reality of participation in Christ and Christ's benefits as we receive the signs with faith. Faith does not cause Christ to be present, but faith is the way we benefit from that presence, enabled by the power of the Holy Spirit. Calvin puts the various dimensions of the Lord's Supper together in a passage that is worth quoting at length:

> To summarize: our souls are fed by the flesh and blood of Christ in the same way that bread and wine keep and sustain physical life. For the analogy of the sign applies only if souls find their nourishment in Christ—which cannot happen unless Christ truly grows into one with us, and refreshes us by the eating of his flesh and the drinking of his blood. Even though it seems unbelievable that Christ's flesh, separated from us by such a great distance, penetrates to us, so that it becomes our food, let us remember how far the secret power of the Holy Spirit towers above all our senses, and how foolish it is to wish to measure his immeasurableness by our measure. What, then, our mind does not comprehend, let faith conceive: that the Spirit truly unites things separated in space. Now, that sacred partaking of his flesh and blood, by which Christ pours his life into us, as if it penetrated into our bones and marrow, he also testifies and seals in the Supper—not by presenting a vain and empty sign, but by manifesting there the effectiveness of his Spirit to fulfill what he promises. And truly he offers and shows the reality there signified to all who sit at that spiritual banquet, although it is received with benefit by believers alone, who accept such generosity with true faith and gratefulness of heart. (*Institutes* 4.17.10)

"The same Spirit who inspired the prophets and apostles rules our faith and life in Christ through Scripture . . ." (lines 58–60) *and calls women and men to all ministries of the Church.* The ministries of the church are ways Christ, the head of the church, orders it by the power of the Spirit according to the written form of the Word. Though that sentence is a mouthful, its components need to be kept together when it comes to considering so important a thing as right church order. Church order is not primarily a question of how to get something done efficiently, though that is part of it. Church order is primarily a matter of believers living together in a way that is congruent with the reality to which the church witnesses, and that—to repeat it once more—is the new life in Christ enabled by the gospel. That new life together, including the structures and offices that serve the accurate and powerful transmission and reinterpretation of the apostolic message, exists as an instrument of service of the Servant Lord. The church's sole authority is its service—that is all the word "ministry" means—of the gospel, though the forms that service takes are manifold. Forms of the church's ministry that are not congruent with the freeing servanthood of Jesus Christ, the head of the church, need correcting.

Line 64 is a confession that contains such a necessary correction. It stands as a correction against the practice of dividing up the ministries of the church between those to which men were called and those to which women were called. That is a centuries-old practice, which can, indeed, claim biblical warrant—especially in the explicit prohibition of "women speaking in church" in some of the Pauline epistles.[4] That prohibition is, however, only one part of the biblical material. (This is a crucial point.) The purpose those passages were intended to serve in a specific cultural context—Paul's struggle with the "spiritualists" in the church at Corinth—may well be better served in other contexts by other provisions.

Tradition takes seriously the principle that scripture is its own best interpreter, in the sense that specific passages are to be understood not in isolation but in context with other parts of the whole. However, that is quite different from excising those parts of scripture which are inconvenient, unpleasant, nonmalleable. That principle justifies the judgment, even out of other Pauline material, that the controlling message of Paul's ministry is inclusive; that the promises made to Abraham and Sarah apply also to the Gentiles, that God's purposes from the beginning are reconciling and expanding, so that believers realize they have been freely reconciled to God and given a ministry of reconciliation. That central message needs to be reflected today, in an ordering of the church that recognizes that women as well as men are gifted by the Holy Spirit for all offices of the church.

Another way of saying the same thing is to say that the composition of the ministries of the church must express the fact that in Christ the image of God into which humans were created has been restored. A church order that refuses to recognize the call of women, as well as men, who are gifted by the Spirit for a specific ministry is a form of denying the restoration of that image. This is the implication of lines 29–32 for the structures and mission of the church: "In sovereign love God created the world good and makes everyone equally in God's image, male and female, of every race and people, to live as one community." The church whose every ministry includes women and men gifted for it by the Spirit is, in its very life together, a witness to God's sovereign love in a broken and fearful world.

Note that line 64 is not saying that the Spirit calls *all* women and men to the ministries of the church. That also is true enough, if one is speaking about evangelism and in the sense that everyone who is baptized shares in a common ministry, the priesthood of all believers. In that sense, every believer's vocation is a form of ministry, of service to Christ and Christ's purposes in the church and in the world. Lines 72–76, as we shall see, are particularly devoted to this dimension of the Christian's life. But line 64 is addressing the more specific forms of the ministry to which persons are ordained, and is saying that not only are women and men called to the common ministry by virtue of their baptism but both women and men are called to the special ministries to which persons so gifted are set apart by ordination.

That is the point at which this Statement makes a distinctive contribution with regard to the ministry—and it is on this

point that it makes a weighty decision affecting ecumenical re-
lations. Confessing line 64 identifies a fundamental conflict
with those denominations which do not yet see their way clear
to ordain women as pastors, priests, bishops—and usually not
as deacons. When we take the ordination vows in the
Presbyterian Church, we promise to study and promote the
peace and unity of the church—so this action of confessing line
64 is not to be easily dismissed or taken lightly. It can be taken
only in the trust that doing so will actually correct practices
that themselves are today adding enormously to destructive
polarization within the church. It can be taken only in the trust
that in doing so we are being led not to some schismatic air of
superiority over other churches but to a shape of the ministry
that belongs to the future catholicity of the church.

12. The Witness of God's People
(Lines 65–71)

65 In a broken and fearful world
66 the Spirit gives us courage
67   to pray without ceasing,
68   to witness among all peoples to Christ as Lord and
            Savior,
69   to unmask idolatries in Church and culture,
70   to hear the voices of peoples long silenced,
71   and to work with others for justice, freedom, and peace.

The Spirit has a *sending* effect on the church. The Spirit's going forth, mission, is the presupposition of creation and new creation. Sharing in the life of the Spirit, the church shares in this mission of the Spirit. The Nicene Creed confesses the church to be "one holy catholic and apostolic." This section deals with the way the church is apostolic, not just in being founded upon and continually reformed according to the message of the original apostles, but in being continually *sent as witness in God's world.*

In a broken and fearful world the Spirit gives us courage. . . . The time and place of the church's witness is this world. Of course the church is drawn forward to, and already shaped by, the sure and lively hope of the new heaven and new earth, whose fullness is still to come (lines 72–76). The church's fidelity in the meantime, however, is lived out in the midst of the conditions that cry out for redemption here and now. The creation still groans in travail awaiting its redemption (see Rom. 8). We share in the life of the Spirit in this world, precisely that Spirit who intercedes for us and who prays on our behalf when we do not know how to pray. That is the location and the dynamic of the church's courageous witness: in the Spirit under the conditions of this world.

This section (lines 65–71) takes the form of one sentence shaped around the central assertion that in this broken and fearful world the Spirit *gives us courage to pray . . . to witness . . . to unmask . . . to hear . . . and to work*. Each aspect of the church's witness in a broken and fearful world entails that particular *courage* which is part of life together in Christ enabled by the Holy Spirit. Courage here does not mean ignorance of the perils inherent in the situation. It means focusing more on the magnitude of grace than on the paralyzing realities of those things, within us and without, which still hold out against God's ultimate benevolence.

This particular courage is a function of the love of the community that overcomes dread-full obstacles, a function of the love that casts out fear by focusing on the goodness of the reality to which one seeks to witness. It is neither pinnacle-leaping heroism, nor the virtue that has a heart pinned on at the end of the yellow brick road, nor self-forgetfulness in hateful destruction of one's enemies. Courage here is the assurance that we are not alone when confronting the enormity of need and injustice, within and without. Courage here is the daily practice of holding fast to Christ's promise not to leave his followers alone but to be with them to the end of the age (Matt. 28:20; and John 14–16).

Instead of grim determination, this courage is that quality of effective freedom which comes from welcoming others as Christ has welcomed us (See Rom. 15:7–13). The welcoming of others includes being part of God's own relentless purposes to establish justice as fully in this world as in heaven. Each just action, no matter how small or seemingly insignificant, no matter how large and fearfully consequential, is a Spirit-enabled act of courage by the freely forgiven sinners who are comembers of the body of Christ.

In a broken and fearful world the Spirit gives us courage to pray without ceasing. . . . It takes courage in a broken and fearful world to pray without ceasing. It takes time and energy, but not courage, to try to escape this world and one's responsibilities in it by substituting false piety for faith active in love. But of course that is counterfeit prayer—incantation for show, divorced from repentance and from helping the poor. We do not need to spend much space on the misuses of prayer (which are many) when the positive calling to genuine prayer is so essential to every other aspect of the Christian life.

Prayer is not one of the many things the Christian community does. Everything that is freely lavished on us through Christ, Calvin says, we are also to ask for through prayer: "Therefore we see that to us nothing is promised to be expected from the Lord, which we are not bidden to ask of him in prayers. So true is it that we dig up by prayer the treasures that were pointed out by the Lord's gospel, and which our faith has gazed upon" (*Institutes* 3.20.2). Prayer informs everything else the Christian does. Prayer is that which continually redirects all we do to the Subject of our trust and the goal of our activity. It is the discipline without which even our best works—no, especially our best activity and our most fervent trust—become ends in themselves which finish us off. In this sense prayer is the continual acknowledgment that all we have is from God, that we are saved by grace, not works, and that we are therefore freed to do the good works prepared beforehand for us to do (Eph. 2:4–10).

Our prayers are not good works which earn God's favor or manipulate a miserly, reluctant divinity. Nor are prayers things we have to go through, things we have to keep up on like extortion payments, in order to fend off God's disfavor. That would be to reintroduce legalism into prayer, and prayer is essentially an act of intimately personal trust practiced by those who know they already belong to God and to one another. Our prayers (to put the matter in terms of Christian freedom) are covered with the garment of Christ's righteousness and for that reason are acceptable to God just as they are, a mixture of the new life in Christ and the sinfulness against which we must strive all our life long (Heidelberg Catechism 4.056).

At the heart of every form of Christian prayer is the act of faith that acknowledges and responds to God's faithfulness. "Prayer rightly begun springs from faith, and faith, from hearing God's Word [Rom. 10:14, 17]" (Calvin, *Institutes* 3.20.27). Christian prayer is talking back to God. It is talking back to God with all the range of emotions and requests that are found in what, after all, was the earliest church's main prayer book and hymnbook—the Psalms. Christian prayer arises from God's addressing us, from the Word which befalls us and redefines our experienced need, from the Word which breaks into the circle of our self-containment and discloses that for which we basically, not just superficially, hunger and are restless. It is in response to God's self-disclosure that we can pray with Augustine: "O Thou who hast created us for thyself, our hearts are restless until they rest in Thee."

Much ink has been spilt, and undoubtedly many appointments missed, in trying to determine what Paul meant by the exhortation in 1 Thessalonians 5:17 to "pray without ceasing" (see also Rom. 1:9, and Eph. 6:18). That phrase has given rise to any number of practices, from one end of the spectrum which resolves the implied difficulty by considering that everything we do is prayer, to the other end of the spectrum which resolves the implied difficulty by considering anything we do except prayer as a necessary but lesser form of discipleship. In its own historical context, Paul's admonition to pray without ceasing most probably referred to the watchfulness which was, and is, to characterize the Christian community's active hope. In any event, to pray without ceasing means to be continually *entrusting* to God's care everything we can conceive of—all we do, all we hope for, all we care for, all we worry about, all we are in solidarity with, all our commissions (sinful and otherwise) and omissions (sinful and otherwise), the whole of creation.

To pray without ceasing is *not* the practice of "letting go" much romanticized by popular posters. Praying without ceasing is the discipline of *committing* to God, turning over to God's care, those things and persons for which prayer is offered. This is true as much of prayers that are thanksgivings as of prayers of petition and intercession. In thanksgiving we are celebrating that for which God has already shown care, the fruits of which we commend to this same gracious God. Such committing to God's care is simultaneously a *commitment* on the part of the person praying, an act of recovenanting love and activity toward those for whom one intercedes and toward those for whom one gives thanks. Prayer and active involvement are not matters of preference; they belong together and are the business of every believer. Prayer is a form of action for the subject of one's prayers, and acts of merciful justice are an indispensable part of acceptable prayer.

To pray without ceasing is not unlike remembering the Sabbath, to keep it holy. Yes, there is one day that is especially set aside for special observance, and this day is not interchangeable with the other days. But this special day's observance colors the way every other day is lived, so the Sabbath observance brings with it a worshiping focus and ethical behavior that transform commonly experienced time into the time of actively remembering God's identity and Israel's identity before God. In the same way, to pray without ceasing is at the head of the things the Spirit gives us courage to do in a broken and fearful world. The prayerful quality of life in the Spirit is present in every other way the believing community witnesses in this world.

In a broken and fearful world the Spirit gives us courage . . . to witness among all peoples to Christ as Lord and Savior. . . . According to Acts, the Holy Spirit enables the disciples to witness when they do not know the times and seasons of the fulfillment of God's purposes. "So when they had come together, they asked him, 'Lord, is this the time when you will restore the kingdom to Israel?' He replied, 'It is not for you to know the times or periods that the Father has set by his own authority. But you will receive power when the Holy Spirit has come upon you; and you will be my witnesses in Jerusalem, in all Judea and Samaria, and to the ends of the earth' " (Acts 1:6–8).

We get our word "martyr" from the Greek word for witness. To witness means to bear public testimony to someone or something, to go on record, as it were, about the truth of something. That does not mean that every form of Christian witness entails what has come to be understood by martyrdom.

It does mean, however, that the Holy Spirit enables us to be Christ's witnesses, calling us thereby to a life of costly discipleship. In some times and seasons, which are in God's hands, the cost of discipleship is persecution unto death. There is full martyrdom today, and there will be full martyrdom in the future— not just in the first centuries, when the blood of the ancients was the seed of the church. In some times and seasons, however, the little-noticed and yet no less precious acts of fidelity in the face of relentless odds are the forms of witness enabled by the Spirit. The church does not seek out martyrdom; and, in fact, that is part of the church's normative prayer, that we be not put to the test: "and lead us not into temptation." But we pray that we will be enabled to stand in the time of testing, that in whatever we do we will be prepared to give a defense for the hope that is in us (see 1 Peter 3:13–18).

The risks of witnessing were not and are not an abstract issue; they can become literally a matter of life and death. During the Roman persecutions, if a person chose to insist on calling Jesus the Christ, Lord and Savior, he or she (or worse, his or her children) would be put to death, often after torture. Or if Christians refused to hand over the church's sacred writings, they faced the same consequences. All a person had to do to escape torture and death was to compromise the faith, turn over the scriptures to the authorities, and reveal the names of other hunted Christians. One of the miracles of the church's continued existence, one of the most telling signs of the mystery of Christ's fidelity to those joined to him by the power of the Spirit, is the fact that believers, ancient and modern, choose to stand up and be counted in the face of enormous persecution, blatant or subtle; choose to deliver the gospel to others (including their persecutors) as good news for them rather than betray the gospel for apparent personal (or familial, or racial, or national, or class) gain.

Evangelism is simply this witnessing to Christ as Lord and Savior in, and for, a broken and fearful world. It—evangelism—is the whole range of the believing community's life together, which is a living testimony to the truth of the gospel.[1] In all its forms, evangelism is truth telling, pointing to the One who is the way, the truth, and the life. While that may seem obvious, the implications of this are sometimes overlooked when it comes to what is often perpetrated under the name of "evangelism." It is quite possible to gain religious success as the world counts success by using threatening and fearful and lustful methods which are themselves betrayals of the very gospel they purport to be advancing.

There is no room for finger pointing here, since we are all subject to the self-deception that leaves our own form of evangelism uncorrected. Everyone who courageously seeks to share the gospel needs to be reminded not just of Peter's betrayal of Christ, but also of Simon the magician, whose story we read in Acts 8. All he, Simon Magus, wanted was to purchase that power of the Holy Spirit so he too could do the mighty acts he thought the apostles were doing. A religious magician, then or now, is just one who misses the point that the Holy Spirit is not a power pack for doing great things, even very successful religious campaigns, as the world counts success, but is simply and strictly what enables the community of believers to point to Christ and his benefits, the results of which are in the hands of God, whom we know to be love.

In a broken and fearful world the Spirit gives us courage . . . to unmask idolatries in Church and culture, to hear the voices of peoples long silenced. . . . These lines are pivotal for understanding the concreteness of the Spirit-enabled activity designated in the previous and in the following lines. Witnessing to Christ as Lord and Savior simply cannot be done without challenging idolatries, simply cannot be done without hearing and pleading the cause of the stifled ones, simply cannot be done without making common cause for justice and freedom and peace.

Undoubtedly the title "lord" has often malfunctioned to undergird oppressive structures. But the true force of Christ's being Lord is to confront and judge and overturn every oppressive substitute for the freedom and accountability of the gospel. That Christ is Lord and Savior does not mean a part-time occupation of caring for part of the lives of a part of creation. Christ is God's claim on the whole of life and the reordering of every relationship there is or was or ever will be. Once again, the words of the Barmen Declaration need to ring in our ears:

As Jesus Christ is God's assurance of the forgiveness of all our sins, so in the same way and with the same seriousness he is also God's mighty claim upon our whole life. Through him befalls us a joyful deliverance from the godless fetters of this world for a free, grateful service to his creatures.

We reject the false doctrine, as though there were areas of our life in which we would not belong to Jesus Christ, but to other lords—areas in which we would not need justification and sanctification through him. (8:14–15)

Witnessing among all peoples to Christ as Lord and Savior *unmask[s] idolatries in church and culture.* This is another place where the concrete relevance, the transforming toughness, of the forgiveness of sins is clear. Too often we treat forgiveness as what one has recourse to in lieu of correcting injustices, whereas forgiveness is an indispensable element in that correction of injustice which does not simply substitute one set of oppressive delusions for another. Love, power, and justice, we were long ago reminded, belong together, and one cannot have any of them without their interplay. Thus the unmasking of idolatries is an intensely reflexive action, and the discerning accuracy of unmasking idols requires that the unmasking prophet recognize in himself or herself the continual need for repentance. Otherwise, with startling abruptness, the unmasking of idolatries itself becomes idolatrous, and the prophet begins to relish the role of unmasker instead of being moved by a vision of the goodness that is the alternative to idolatries.

An earlier version of the Brief Statement of Faith, the one originally circulated to congregations for their suggestions, had a different version of this line. That earlier version spoke of "smash[ing] the idols of church and culture." At first sight, the present amended version (which speaks of unmasking idolatries in church and culture) seems too mild. It appears to use a weaker verb, and, more seriously, it seems to minimize the power of idols (which are more than idolatries). On further reflection, however, we see an important wisdom in the reaction of congregations who took exception to the original formulation. "Smashing" connoted violence just when the church must witness to its opposite; smashing idols sounded like an additional contribution to the brokenness and fearfulness of the world.

Moreover—and this is not a minor point—a persistent strain of iconoclasm has marked the Reformed churches, and not infrequently that iconoclasm ran amok. Our forebears smashed up statues and broke up stained-glass windows in the name of their reforming faith. In attending to the Second Commandment, the overarching commandment of love sometimes got muted.

"To unmask idolatries in Church and culture" has the advantage of making the problem much clearer and nearer to home. We could be deluded into thinking that idols are relics of remote religious history, from which we suppose ourselves to be free because we worship in sanctuaries swept clean of perfidious images by puritan forebears! But idolatries in church and culture are a different matter. None can escape the glare of contrast between the living God, who frees and makes alive, and the convenient loyalties, which bind and lull into deathly complacency.

The drawing power of idolatries is precisely their usefulness, their convenience, their controllability, their malleability for the ends of our own designing. Their seriousness derives from our seriously looking to them for the real help we need, which has to do with enabling righteousness and freedom and peace and forgiveness. One of the most devastating ways the biblical material attacks idols and idolatries is by mocking their claims. They cannot be relied on to guide and support their worshipers; they are deadweights, portable gods for show. In Isaiah, the Lord comforts the remnant of Israel by reminding them that he has carried them from their birth and will continue to do so when they are old: "I have made, and I will bear; I will carry and will save" (Isa. 46:4). Such care is in sharp contrast to what those get who pay a goldsmith for a custom-made idol. "They lift it to their shoulders, they carry it,/they set it in its place, and it stands there;/it cannot move from its place./If one cries out to it, it does not answer/or save anyone from trouble" (Isa. 46:7). The idols are convenient for campfires; they can be carved, broken for firewood, and replaced with newer models. Where the living God restores humans to the image in which they were created, idols make people into clones of what they worship— disposable, consumable, useful things. In the words of the psalmist:

> They [the idols] have hands, but do not feel;
>> feet, but do not walk;
>>> they make no sound in their throats.
> Those who make them are like them;
>> so are all who trust in them.
> O Israel, trust in the Lord!
>>>> (Ps. 115:7–9a)

In a broken and fearful world the Spirit gives us courage . . . to hear the voices of peoples long silenced, and to work with others for justice, freedom, and peace (lines 65–66, 70–71). These lines belong so closely together that we may treat them in one section. Line 70 is pivotal for understanding the preceding and the following lines. It points to the criterion the prophets persistently used to tell the difference between idolatrous forms of "justice, freedom, and peace" and the freedom, justice, and peace of the living God. Whatever the ultimate destiny of the mighty who drown out the voices of the poor, scripture identifies God as the Holy One who hears and delivers those who have none other to plead their cause. God does indeed pay attention to the mighty, but not in the way they grow accustomed to supposing. As the Magnificat reminds us, God is the One who looks on the lowliness of God's servant, and remembers God's promises:

> "The Mighty One has done great things for me,
>> and holy is his name.
> His mercy is for those who fear him
>> from generation to generation.
> He has shown strength with his arm;
>> he has scattered the proud in the thoughts
>>> [KJV, "imagination"] of their hearts.
> He has brought down the powerful from their thrones,
>> and lifted up the lowly;
> he has filled the hungry with good things,
>> and sent the rich away empty."
>>>> (Luke 1:49–53)

The graceful reversal of the condition of the poor is strikingly put in Flannery O'Connor's short story "Revelation." Mrs. Turpin and her husband, Claude, are in the doctor's office more or less minding their business, when all of a sudden she gets hit with a phone book and called a racist old sow by a Wellesley student who has come home South for the summer. Mrs. Turpin deeply resents this attack, if for no other reason than that she and Claude have always tried to be good in the social setting allotted them—namely, not as wealthy white folk, not as black folk, and especially not as white trash. The anger over the accusation (the conflict set in motion is part of the revelation) so works on Mrs. Turpin that she finally attacks the pigs in the pen on her farm, punishing them with cleanliness from a hose whether they like it or not. And then above the rails of the pigpen she sees a vision, a purple streak in the sky.

> She saw the streak as a vast swinging bridge extending upward from the earth through a field of living fire. There were whole companies of white trash, clean for the first time in their lives, and bands of black niggers in white robes, and battalions of freaks and lunatics shouting and leaping like frogs. And bringing up the end of the procession was a tribe of people whom she recognized at once as those who, like herself and Claude, had always had a little of everything and the God-given wit to use it right. She leaned forward to observe them closer. They were marching behind the others with great dignity, accountable as they had always been for good order and common sense and respectable behavior. They alone were on key. Yet she could see by their shocked and altered faces that even their virtues were being burned away.[2]

The primary motivation believers have for hearing the voices of those long silenced is one of identity: being united by the bond of the Spirit to Christ is a matter of sharing in his compassionate identification with and ministry to those who have none to plead their cause. It is precisely in knowing and hearing the voice of this Shepherd that believers know to hear and to take action on behalf of the voices of those long silenced. Those voices, any human voices, are not inherently and on their own revelatory either of the goodness God intends for all humans or of the depth of the human predicament. The community that knows the normative narrative of God's steadfastness inevitably engages in an actively interpretive hearing, and a deliberate seeking out to hear as yet unnoticed voices.[3] Hearing the voices of the unrepresented, the crowded out, those who have none to care for them is at the heart of the gospel, at the heart of Christ's own ministry, and at the heart of the ministry of those who are bound together in a common life by the power of the Spirit. The social setting of this gospel is primarily that of the marginalized, rejected, or, worse, simply ignored persons (not exclusively, though, because the privileged too can discover that they are entrapped by the structures of oppression). The presence of the new reign of God has centrally to do with a reversal of the condition of these people.

We have said something about the Spirit's encouraging us to hear those voices because we are united to the One whose ministry is primarily (not exclusively) to such people. Now we must say the same thing but in a different way, namely, by calling attention to the work of the Holy Spirit in making those voices heard. We are helped to hear more sensitively and faithfully; but the Holy Spirit is also at work in bringing those voices to expression. The Holy Spirit is at once the *bond* that unites us to Christ the Servant Lord and the *Advocate* ("Paraclete") who speaks up for the defenseless and persecuted.

In John 14–16, the Spirit is promised as the Advocate (which is a more accurate translation than "Comforter"), one who speaks up for, makes the case on behalf of, someone. In the context of John's Gospel, the disciples are being prepared not just for their grief at Jesus' death, though that is part of the story, but also for finding themselves persecuted and weak in the midst of the world and yet commissioned to the ministry of serving after the manner of their Servant Lord. The disciples' condition reflects the true condition of the church in the world, the world that is still the object of God's love, but which measures weakness and power quite differently from what the gospel commends.[4] The community that is moved to trust the gospel as applying even to itself is the community that is committed to hearing the voices of other downtrodden people—and moved to being a community of advocacy on their behalf. They are a community of advocacy because they are indwelt by, freed by, moved by the Holy Spirit, who is Advocate. Christian advocacy is not founded on anything so marshy as changing political climates or quickly soured idealisms. Christian advocacy is founded on the identity of the God to whom all persons belong, to whom the whole creation belongs, whose steadfast love will ultimately have its way against the most vociferous worldly opposition.

In the social placement and time of the Brief Statement of Faith, there are some obvious voices long silenced, and some not so obvious ones. Surely those voices include those of women inside and outside the church; minorities in our culture—African Americans, Hispanics, Asians, native Americans, the Appalachian white; the handicapped, by whatever name; the aged; and the children, some of whom come into the world with cocaine or the AIDS virus in their system and with no prospect of a drug-free or crime-free future. Cutting across all these groups are the multitude of economically disadvantaged, whose plight is evident in homelessness, inadequate health care, poor education, class discrimination, immobility from their mind- and body-warping fatigue and malnutrition. And this is just a partial, very selective index of the voices that need attending in the North American context.

The magnitude of the demands, however, is so much greater when seen in the perspective of our global setting and accountability. Even with internal needs it leaves unfulfilled, North American society consumes a shockingly disproportionate amount of the globe's total present and foreseeable resources. Marshall McLuhan spoke of the "global village" to call attention to the effect of modern media on awareness of our interconnectedness; but "village" does not do justice to the complexity, size, unpredictability of the geopolitical nexus in which all peoples today are caught. Part of what we experience as the brokenness and fear of the contemporary world is the threatening complexity, magnitude, and arbitrariness of things on such a scale. Yet in this global context the church is committed to hearing the voices of those long (and even recently) silenced. These are the voices of those caught in famine on an enormous scale in Ethiopia (to take only one example), the voices of those caught up in the inter- and intraracial violence in South Africa, the voices of the poor in Latin American countries who are economically dependent on an international drug industry, the voices of those who languish in dying places for AIDS victims in Africa and elsewhere, the voices of Palestinian refugees who endure the most blatant injustices and are lumped together as terrorists, the cries of those who must witness the destruction of their unique culture at the hands of rapacious developers, and so on. The list is not exhaustive—and that is the point. As each set of voices is heard, those previously muted people need to be freed to take their turn in helping us hear and do something about others who have none to speak up for them.

We cannot turn to the next section without mentioning another dimension of the care for which the Spirit gives the church courage in a broken and fearful world. I think, of course, of the *long-silenced voices of those who are not people.* Part of the work of the Holy Spirit is the recovery of the right relationship among all participants in the whole of creation. Only a myopically anthropocentric view of creation and redemption could fail to grasp the interconnection of human destiny and the future of the planet and even outer space.

Those who have no voice in the human forum need persons to speak up for them, need persons to protect them from abuse and extinction. There is a good reason for including the elaborate provisions for caring for animals in the book of Leviticus; a crassness toward other parts of creation is symptomatic of a basic disregard of the fact that none of creation finally belongs to humans, but all belongs to God. It is one thing to evaluate the place of this or that animal for this or that labor or nourishment—or for mutual comfort and fun! It is one thing to follow this or that practice of work in order to provide periods of rest for beasts and humans alike. It is quite another thing for people whose entertainment is the rapacious destruction of other species, whose thrills entail the wanton consumption of minerals and plants, whose engineering ignores the delicate balances among the entities they are handling, to "use" creation for human ends. The latter violates the distinctive place every creature, inanimate and otherwise, has before the face of God. All of creation belongs to God!

The Brief Statement of Faith says that the Spirit gives us courage to *work with others for justice, freedom, and peace.* The mission of the church, as described in this section (lines 65–71), is overwhelming if it is taken seriously. It is so overwhelming that it can engender the opposite of active hearing—paralyzing discouragement or hardness of heart or rationalized privilege. That is why it is essential to recall that the courage being spoken of is the gift of the Holy Spirit, and as such includes but goes far beyond any reasonable expectation of being able to fulfill all the righteousness that being God's people in such a broken and fearful world demands. That placement, being before a righteous God, overwhelmed with the question of how to be righteous—in this case, how to hear and correct the plight of the voices of those long silenced—is not a new one for believers. It is just a new form of being placed before God, who is not kidding about the demands of the law given for the covenantal well-being of God's people and for the whole of creation. The curse of the law is that it is self-defeating, by inducing sloth instead of joyful service in that particular area in which one can, indeed, make a positive difference.

Part of the way the Spirit gives us courage to hear the voices of the long-silenced is *through working with others* for freedom, justice, and peace. Otherwise, what starts out as a humble and courageous service of others becomes a messianic complex on the loose, to the harm of others and self. In *this* world, broken and fearful, the freedom, justice, and peace for which we are encouraged to cooperate are imperfect and penultimate. We are drawn forward by the vision of a perfection that is only partially and anticipatorily tasted already here and now. That being drawn forward to the ultimate fullness of freedom, justice, and peace does not mean despairing quietude. It means *work* and it means work *with others*.

The church is not being true to its own calling when it despairs in the face of the magnitude of the task to be done, nor is the church being true to its identity when it so covets its purity that it refuses to make common cause, for this and that season, and with this and that critical distance, with other movements for penultimate expressions of freedom, justice, and peace. The reason for this cooperation for penultimate good is, finally, not the church's own disposition or choice or intent. The reason is that the church, and those with whom the church is freed to work and those on whose behalf common cause is being made, belong to God, whose love extends to all and who is already at work through other means than the church. God is already at work in the world, as Paul Lehmann puts it, to make and keep human life human; and the church is that fellowship which discerns and freely joins in God's worldly work.[5]

13. Joyful Perseverance (Lines 72–76)

72   In gratitude to God, empowered by the Spirit,
73   we strive to serve Christ in our daily tasks
74   and to live holy and joyful lives,
75   even as we watch for God's new heaven and new earth,
76   praying, "Come, Lord Jesus!"

These lines (72–76), on joyful fidelity in daily vocations, and the lines on justification by grace alone within the body of Christ (lines 54–57), bracket what the Brief Statement says about the Spirit's work in gathering (lines 58–64) and in sending (lines 65–71) the church. The whole is an explication of the third part of trust in the one triune God: *We trust in God the Holy Spirit, everywhere the giver and renewer of life* (lines 52–53). The *Christian life* is fundamentally joyful because it is one of trust—in life and in death—in the One who is everywhere the giver and renewer of *life.* This trust is *grateful* because it is based on what God has already done, and it is *watchful* because it is drawn forward in anticipation of the completion of God's benevolent purposes. Watchful gratitude, grateful expectation—these are the components of striving *to serve Christ in our daily tasks and to live holy and joyful lives.* In a broken and sinful world we are *empowered by the Spirit* in the priesthood of all believers.

Sheer endurance is never a simple thing, and is not to be despised. But the perseverance of the saints is something more—it is a gift of the Spirit which has a positive, forward-looking goal:

the newness of life. That newness of life is already experienced in the present, no matter how minuscule and apparently fragile the present intimation of the coming glory may be. From our present, partial experience of it, we know that what is to come is incomparably greater and more glorious, goes far beyond what we can even dream. That is why the language of hope is richly poetic. Think only of the overlapping metaphors in the book of Revelation. There we find cascading imagery upon imagery of the Lamb once slain and now on the throne, to whom all honor and power and wisdom and might are ascribed by vast choruses of persons clothed in white, from whose eyes all tears have been wiped away as they celebrate in a bejeweled city the defeat of the many-headed beast! This is apocalyptic language; but what is being expressed there hyperbolically is the solid truth of tough, ordinary, everyday Christian hope. Hope means being engaged in present transformative action in view of what is to come.

The African American tradition has expressed this transformative hope with a special power. Its spirituals are not consoling substitutes for hope of deliverance but active means of hope, strong equipment for keeping alive the vision of God's alternative to the devilry of slavery. And they are strong equipment for keeping alive the vision of God's alternative to the continuing perversity of racial discrimination long after the official emancipation of enslaved persons. The songs of the civil rights movement and the preaching of Christian African Americans are specific instances of how the Spirit empowers people to serve Christ in their daily tasks and to live holy and joyful lives, lives watchful for God's new heaven and earth, lives that sing out, "Come, Lord Jesus!"

One of Martin Luther King, Jr.'s, great sermons, entitled "A Knock at Midnight," is based on Luke 11:5–7. He does not *say* anything in that sermon—he *announces*. Doctor King announces that:

> The church today is challenged to proclaim God's Son, Jesus Christ, to be the hope of men [and women] in all of their complex personal and social problems. . . . Midnight is a confusing hour when it is difficult to be faithful. The most inspiring word that the church may speak is that no midnight long remains. The weary traveller by midnight who asks for bread is really

seeking the dawn. Our eternal message of hope is that dawn will come. Our slave foreparents realized this. They were never unmindful of the fact of midnight, for always there was the rawhide whip of the overseer and the auction block where families were torn asunder to remind them of its reality. . . . Encompassed by a staggering midnight but believing that morning would come they sang:

> I'm so glad trouble don't last alway.
> O my Lord, O my Lord, what shall I do?

Their positive belief in the dawn was the growing edge of hope that kept the slaves faithful amid the most barren and tragic circumstances.

Faith in the dawn arises from the faith that God is good and just. When one believes this, he [or she] knows that the contradictions of life are neither final nor ultimate. He [or she] can walk through the dark night with the radiant conviction that all things must work together for good for those that love God. Even the most starless midnight may herald the dawn of some great fulfillment.[1]

In gratitude and watchfulness enabled by the Spirit, believers strive to serve Christ in their daily tasks. This is *the vocation of the priesthood of all believers.* The recovery of the sacredness of every believer's work was a special contribution of the Reformation. That contribution came as a protest against the view that there were some tasks that were inherently holier than others. By the late Middle Ages it was common to think that there was a vast difference between the common work done by the laity, who dealt with temporal things, and the sacred work done by priests, who dealt with what really counted—the holy things through which we come to eternal life. In his ordination, the priest was given the power, not just legitimation, necessary for the sacraments to be efficacious. Emergency baptism could be done by a layperson, such as the midwife. But it was only the priest who had the power to marry people so they would not be living in sin and bearing illegitimate children and unable to come to Mass; it was only the priest who had the power to speak the words of absolution on which depended one's endless future in heaven or hell; it was only the priest who had the power to say the words without which there was no sacrifice of the Mass.

Luther's breakthrough was primarily the rediscovery that the gospel is freely proclaimed and that we are justified by grace alone. That breakthrough utterly altered the prevailing understanding of the power of the priesthood and utterly altered what was considered sacred. Luther contended that the priest's power is simply and exclusively that of announcing the good news through preaching and the sacraments. The good news freely announced contains the call to repentance and it contains the assurance of pardon. No indulgences or other works of satisfaction are required for the absolution of one's sin, and the only merits to be considered are Christ's. Men and women thus freely forgiven exercise their sacred calling in what they do—be it shoemaker, farmer, homemaker, soldier, teacher, miner, scholar, barber. Each person's workbench is his or her altar, each person is freed to be good at what he or she does, and each person is accountable to be a faithful steward.[2]

Every insight is exposed to misunderstanding, and the doctrine of the priesthood of all believers is no exception. It sometimes got coupled with an interpretation of "Honor your father and your mother," which got twisted to mean abject submission to the authorities no matter what—knowing your place and staying there in rigid immobility. The Christian understanding of vocation does not mean romanticizing labor; it does not mean minimizing the alienating effects of mass production; it does not mean having any illusions about the dehumanizing drudgery of that kind of work which only perpetuates one's place below the poverty level. For vast numbers of people around the world today, labor still means a losing battle with bone-crushing fatigue, just to survive in order to care for one's family one more day and night.

But the basic truth of the priesthood of all believers must not be relinquished or ignored just because the idea has been abused. We need to recover the sense of a sacred calling in our mundane work. The priesthood of all believers is the opposite of the nonpriesthood of everyone! We need to recover the meaning of vocation, the sense that in our daily work we are responding to a *calling from God*. Fidelity in the face of boredom, of social pressure, of the sense of being taken for granted, of incessant strain, of pain, of terminal illness—fidelity in the face of these and similar odds is an active reminder to ourselves and to others that also in our work we belong not to ourselves, not to others, but to God. Fidelity in the little things is of enormous consequence in the larger scheme of things. Such perseverance is the acted-out confession that the world belongs to a benevolently reliable God, to whom the little things of beauty count for much.

Though it is often a struggle to do so, to treat our daily work as a vocation is to take a positive action. Taking that action helps us experience the freedom of being engaged in work that is of worth before God, counts in God's eyes, and has dignity contrary to worldly appraisal. It helps free us for effective service in what otherwise seems only to be something imposed on us from without. A dramatic instance of this appears in the theologian Dietrich Bonhoeffer's letters from prison. After the Nazis arrested Bonhoeffer, the prison guards imposed a harsh confinement and punitive schedule on him, but Bonhoeffer interpreted the regimen as the place and practice of his vocation, for that specific time and place, and transformed the prison hours into the framework of the daily offices—and in doing so exercised a remarkable ministry to the prison staff.

In gratitude to God, empowered by the Spirit, we strive to serve Christ in our daily tasks and to live holy and joyful lives. . . . Actually the connection between holiness and joy is a good deal stronger than this wording might suggest. Persevering in grateful expectation is not simply both holy and joyful; it is holy and therefore joyful. Putting it the other way around is also true, namely, that true joy is delight in doing the will of God (see Ps. 119:24, 77, 143–144). Joy arises from focusing on the goodness and beauty of who God is and what God does. A prayer in the language of antiquity puts it nicely:

O Heavenly Father, who hast filled the world with beauty;
Open, we beseech Thee, our eyes to behold Thy gracious hand
in all thy works; that, rejoicing in Thy whole creation, we may
learn to serve Thee with gladness; for the sake of Him by whom
all things were made, Thy Son Jesus Christ, our Lord.[3]

Happiness is also God-given and to be received with gratitude; but joy is greater and deeper than happiness. Joy belongs
to blessedness, because it is oriented toward the Highest
Good. Joy is a celebrative focus on the ultimate benevolence of
God which does not continually count the cost of perseverance. Joy is such a pervasive quality of holiness that it has a certain selflessness about it, a certain élan of admiration and
wonderment, not after or apart from adversity, but through
and in the midst of the plight that befalls our common humanity. That piety is joyless, and hence unholy, which is fixated on
sackcloth and ashes for display.

One of John Ciardi's poems is a healthy booster shot to remind us that our holiness and joy ought at least to exceed
pagan fortitude:

In Place of a Curse

At the next vacancy for God, if I am elected,
I shall forgive last the delicately wounded
who, having been slugged no harder than anyone else,
never got up again, neither to fight back,
nor to finger their jaws in painful admiration.

They who are wholly broken, and they in whom
mercy is understanding, I shall embrace at once
and lead to pillows in heaven. But they who are
the meek by trade, baiting the best of their betters
with the extortions of a mock-helplessness

I shall take last to love, and never wholly.
Let them all into Heaven—I abolish Hell—
but let it be read over them as they enter:
"Beware the calculations of the meek, who gambled nothing,
gave nothing, and could never receive enough."[4]

Fortunately, there is no vacancy for God, that position
being taken by the electing God, who loves wholly. The identity of the One to whom we belong is the ultimate reason for
living holy and joyful lives *even as we watch for God's new
heaven and new earth, praying, "Come, Lord Jesus!"* The church
is not "open to the future" in general. There are some possible

scenarios that the church is definitely opposed to—with the sure knowledge and motivating hope that ultimately destructive futures, including endless extension of the present status quo, are not what God intends to bring about. The church is open to, and actively engaged in helping shape that future which vindicates the steadfast love of the God already known and already decisively triumphant through the death and resurrection of Christ, to whom we are already joined by the bond of the Spirit. It is *God's* new heaven and earth for which the Holy Spirit empowers us to watch.

We do not know the details of the new heaven and new earth or the timing of their arrival. What we do know is that there is both continuity and radical discontinuity between our present experience of heaven and earth and the new heaven and new earth for which we watch. How radical an apocalyptic change one looks for seems to be a function of how incomplete, painful, and fragmentary the present world is as one experiences it. In any event, the church is drawn forward by its vision of the whole of creation (heaven and earth) being healed, corrected, transformed, made just and peaceful. The continuity and discontinuity are not postulated out of nothing: they are known to be features of the new heaven and new earth because of where our hope is focused, on Christ. The same One who was crucified, this same One God raised from the dead. Salvation depends on there being a continuity between the One who was crucified and buried and the One who was raised and will come again (Acts 1:11). The same person is referred to when the church confesses the mystery of its faith: "Christ has died, Christ is risen, Christ will come again."

"Come, Lord Jesus!" What, exactly, are we praying for with these words? We know exactly for *whose return* we are praying, but we do not know literally for *what kind of return* we are praying. We do know enough, however, to pray that prayer in all seriousness and urgency. This can be an honest prayer, because we know at least four things it involves.

We know, first, that Christ's coming again in glory "to judge the living and the dead" will be a far greater reality, will be far more unmistakable in its correcting and vindicating accomplishment, than can be encompassed by any single literal prediction of it. The problem of reducing the event to the level of literal depiction is that such literalness is an effort to control and restrict it to only one set of meanings. Recognizing the errors of literalness, however, tends to take too many of us off the hook, so to speak, for we are thereby tempted to think that by dimissing a crudely literal version of the Second Coming we will be able to escape the inevitable reality of the event itself. All the different images have at least this in common: that nothing and no one will fall outside the manifest, revealed, patent completion of God's creating and redeeming purposes.

We know, second, that we are praying for an event in which we will be held accountable. This is the ultimate and manifest consummation of the good news—and that good news's completion (not ending, but fulfillment) includes the accountability that is part of Christian freedom. We are finally accountable before the throne of grace of Christ who comes again, whose reign will be without end. Christ's return promises to be more than a subjectively interpreted projection on our part. Christ's return promises to be more than the glossing over of injustice. Christ's return promises to be more than enabling people to feel right about doing whatever has been important to their personal satisfaction. Christ's return promises to be more than thanking with a watch and a retirement dinner those who have struggled to live out the cost of discipleship joyfully. Christ's return promises to be an accounting of whether we have cared for the poor and hungry and thirsty and sick and imprisoned. And, of course, who shall stand in that great and glorious day, trusting in his or her own inherent righteousness, his or her record of caring? None!

We know, third, that it is by grace that forgiven sinners care for others, and it is by grace that they can dare to "look forward" to Christ's coming again. For all the awesomely disclosive, unmasking, character of the event, it will be revelatory above all of the One whom we already know to be the great lover of our souls and bodies, the One who took upon himself our judgment, the One whose death and resurrection already broke the back of whatever we would otherwise ultimately have to fear. We awaken to the face of the One we know loves us, and loves our loved ones, and loves our enemies, in fact, loves the whole world with a love that finally will not let go. The

One who comes again is the One in whom our lives are already hidden, the One to whom we are joined by the bond of the Spirit, in short, the One to whom we belong in life and in death. We know what we are praying for because we know the answer to the following question:

Q.1. What is your only comfort in life and in death?

A. That I belong—body and soul, in life and in death—not to myself but to my faithful Savior, Jesus Christ, who at the cost of his own blood has fully paid for all my sins and has completely freed me from the dominion of the devil; that he protects me so well that without the will of my Father in heaven not a hair can fall from my head; indeed, that everything must fit his purpose for my salvation. Therefore, by his Holy Spirit, he also assures me of eternal life, and makes me wholeheartedly willing and ready from now on to live for him (Heidelberg Catechism 4.001)

We know, fourth, that Christ's coming again is *more of the same*—more of the same reality we participate in every time we celebrate the Lord's Supper. That means simply that in all dimensions of their life together in Christ, believers are united to the One who has come and will come again. The gift of the Holy Spirit is *not* what we get *instead of* Christ's presence until he comes again; Christ's coming again does *not* mean he is absent between the ascension and the second coming. The church is the congregation to whom Christ is present as their active head, the One to whom they attend especially through the ordinary means of grace. In the Lord's Supper, Christ's already presence is experienced in such a way as to anticipate Christ's yet-to-come presence. That is why the church considers the Lord's Supper an eschatological feast, why in the Lord's Supper we are showing forth the Lord's death "until he comes," why we give a eucharistic setting to the words "Blessed is he who comes in the name of the Lord." Those who are gathered by Christ around his Table, those who are united to him already by the bond of the Spirit, those forgiven sinners who come to be nourished by this bread for another day's journey, are an effective sign of what God wills for the whole of creation.

Conclusion

14. Hope and Glory
(Lines 77–80)

77   With believers in every time and place,
78   we rejoice that nothing in life or in death
79   can separate us from the love of God in Christ Jesus
             our Lord.

80   Glory be to the Father, and to the Son, and to the Holy
             Spirit. Amen.*

*Instead of saying this line, congregations may wish to sing a version of the Gloria.

A Brief Statement of Faith begins by affirming that we belong to God both in life and in death. All sorts of forces in the world can kill us, from a criminal who assaults us on a city street to a virus, to the engines of warfare and their masters, to the bad luck that puts us accidentally in the path of an oncoming car. If God were only to be trusted for this life, then all those forces would be, where our lives are concerned, potentially more powerful than God. But we really trust in God; we see no need to worship and serve other lords—and that means we trust in a God from whose love we cannot be separated even by death.

Christians have thought about hope that reaches beyond death in two broadly different ways. The conclusion of the Christological section of this Statement (lines 23–26) emphasizes one of them: the belief that "God raised this Jesus from the dead, . . . delivering us from death to life eternal" (lines 23, 26). That is, first of all, a hope for each of us as an individual, that we will share in the good news of Jesus' resurrection. The conclusion of the Statement's section on the Holy Spirit focuses on a different emphasis, the hope for the transformation of the world: "We watch for God's new heaven and new earth, praying, 'Come, Lord Jesus!' " (lines 75–76).

The reason for mentioning these two different emphases is to insist that authentic Christian hope must include them both. If we focus only on the individual side, then our hope comes to be that God will pluck *us* out of this evil world and leave the world to "go to hell." Push that view one step farther, and we start to think that what happens in and to this world does not really matter—after all, we are just waiting to be freed from it. But Christians need to believe that this world does matter, that we should work to make it a better place, that God cares about it, and that God has a plan for the transformation of the world. The author of the book of Revelation envisioned it:

> Then I saw a new heaven and a new earth. . . . And I heard a loud voice from the throne saying,
>
> > "See, the home of God is among mortals.
> > He will dwell with them as their God;
> > they will be his peoples,
> > and God himself will be with them;
> > he will wipe every tear from their eyes.
> > Death will be no more;
> > mourning and crying and pain will be no more."
>
> (Rev. 21:1–4)

On the other hand, if we emphasize only the transformation of the world, we can lose the importance of the individual. Marxists and nationalists of various kinds, for instance, believe that the victory of their nation or the triumph of the working class will make the whole world a better place. In the course of the struggle, some people may have to die, sacrificed for the common good. Push *that* view one step farther and it implies that individuals do not ultimately matter very much and can be sacrificed to whatever strikes us as a good cause. But Christian faith teaches that we are not sacrificed to some larger divine plan, for God's plan rests on God's love for each one of us.

> "Are not five sparrows sold for two pennies? Yet not one of them is forgotten in God's sight. But even the hairs of your head are all counted. Do not be afraid; you are of more value than many sparrows." (Luke 12:6–7)

We trust, therefore, that God has a plan for the universe, and that it is a plan in which neither all the rest of the universe nor we ourselves will be cast aside. In the end, Karl Barth wrote, nothing escapes God:

> No aspect of the great game of creation; no moment of human life; no thinking thought; no word spoken . . . no suffering or joy . . . no ray of sunlight; no note which has ever sounded, no color which has ever been revealed, possibly in the darkness of oceanic depths where the eye of man has never perceived it; no wing-beat of the day-fly in the far flung epochs of geological time. Everything will be present to Him exactly as it was or is or will be, in all its reality, in the whole temporal course of its activity. . . . He will not allow anything to perish, but will hold it in the hollow of his hand as He has always done, and does, and will do. He will not be alone in eternity, but with the creature.[1]

That is the good news, that *nothing . . . can separate us from the love of God in Christ Jesus our Lord.*

And so we should *rejoice.* We Presbyterians are often not very good at rejoicing; many of the standard jokes about Presbyterianism, in fact, have to do with a reputation for a certain stuffiness. As we conclude our confession, therefore, it may be especially important to strike this note of joy. Our chief end, in the words of the Westminster Shorter Catechism, "is to glorify God, and to enjoy him forever" (7.001). To *enjoy!* If we trust in this God, we can live with confidence, we can take pleasure in God's creation. To be sure, as earlier lines of this Brief Statement remind us, we do live "in a broken and fearful world"; we have to "strive" and "work," to "watch" and "pray." But the Christian life should not be as grim a business as such language might suggest. We sing—we "make a joyful noise to the Lord"—and if sometimes it comes out very much

a "noise," what matters is that it be joyful. We weep and struggle together with fellow Christians, but we also laugh together.

If we think of days spent in hard work, even if it was only
the summer project of a church youth group, we often remember what fun we had. If we think of the lives of people who
have struggled hardest in trying to serve God in this broken
and fearful world of ours, their lives often manifest a kind of
delight. If we were earning our salvation, it would no doubt be
a solemn business indeed. But we have been saved; we are responding in gratitude and celebration, and there is plenty of
room for joy.

Moreover, we rejoice together *with believers in every time
and place*. When we stand to confess our faith, we face the joy
and the challenge that we are confessing it together with saints
and martyrs through the centuries, with Ethiopian Christians
facing starvation, with heroic South African Christians struggling against apartheid, and with people in our own communities with whom we might think in any other context that we
had very little in common. We have to think about what it
means that we confess a common faith.

We also confess together with Christians who owned slaves,
Christians who murdered Jews in pogroms, Christians who oppressed and oppress women, Christians who abuse their wives
and children, Christians who use drugs, Christians full of all
sorts of hate and prejudice. That fact reminds us as vividly as
anything could that this confession does not automatically turn
us into morally good people or enable us to see the truth un-
clouded. No doubt other Christians will look back on some of
our actions and beliefs with horror and astonishment. To say
that we are justified by grace through faith (line 54) is to remind ourselves, as we confess our faith, of how much sinners
like us need that grace.

Our confession, however, should not end with a word about
us, even about our salvation and our hope. It ought to end
with the praise of God: *Glory be to the Father, and to the Son,
and to the Holy Spirit. Amen.* We do not worship and serve
God because of all the good things God has done or will do for
us; we worship and serve God because God deserves worship

and service. One old Calvinist ideal was that one should be willing to be "damned for the greater glory of God." God loves us with a sovereign love, and so is not asking for volunteers for damnation, and Calvin always properly warned against the dangers of speculating about hypothetical problems. So that old ideal embodies a risky train of thought. But, however misguidedly, it points to something true. *Our* happiness, even *our* salvation, is not the ultimate goal of things. The ultimate goal of things is the glory of God. So at the end of our confession, we do not celebrate our own rewards, but stand before God "lost in wonder, love, and praise."

This Statement praises God's glory in this traditional Trinitarian form. We affirm yet once more our trust in the triune God, and the Statement here does so in very traditional language. It is not a line to be considered in isolation. As noted earlier in this commentary, the Statement as a whole reflects as best it can our denomination's current sense concerning language about God. We try to introduce new images for God, in saying that God is like a mother. We avoid male pronouns for God, and minimize the application of other male language to God. When we speak of the God whom Jesus called Father, we remember that the word Jesus apparently used was "Abba," with all its challenge to traditional patriarchal images. But, on the other hand, we acknowledge that certain traditional formulations—for instance, baptism "in the name of the Father and of the Son and of the Holy Spirit"—continue, for a variety of reasons, to be part of our life as a church. As a community looking for alternative language, we acknowledge that we have not yet found any that we generally find so completely satisfactory that we can simply dispense with this language. We try, as the Confession of 1967 put it, to bear "a present witness to God's grace in Jesus Christ," remembering that "No one type of confession is exclusively valid, no one statement is irreformable" (9.01, 9.03). Twenty years ago, we would have confessed our faith differently, and no doubt twenty years from now we will be exploring new ways of confessing. But nothing in our life together is more important than our confession of faith, and few things are more important than our struggle to confess our faith *together*. We cannot postpone our confession until we find all the right answers or until all manage to agree. We live in a broken and fearful world, and we are ourselves often broken and fearful. We can only trust that the Spirit gives us courage to confess our faith, however inadequately, not to our own glory, but to the glory of God.

On Asterisks and What It Means to Stand in a Tradition

This Statement of Faith concludes with an alternative: "Instead of saying this [the last] line, congregations may wish to sing a version of the Gloria." Part of the point is obvious: We end with the praise of God, and praise means celebration, means joy, means making the most joyful noise we can manage to our God. Why not sing it?

But there's another point too: "*a* version of *the* Gloria." Some congregations sing a Gloria that avoids the masculine language of Father and Son. Would that be an appropriate replacement?

The Statement itself does not and finally cannot answer such a question. For that matter, we might as well be honest: Some Presbyterian congregations will be using parts of this Statement in all sorts of ways, and rewriting as they go along. Some Presbyterian congregations will not be using it at all. In our tradition, "God alone is Lord of the conscience, and hath left it free from the doctrines and commandments of men which are in anything contrary to his Word, or beside it in matters of faith or worship" (Westminster Confession 6.109). We all have to confess our faith in a way that is honest to who we, as individuals, are.

But part of who we are is that we stand in a tradition, and we stand as part of a church community larger than any given congregation. We confess *with believers in every time and place*. We should not ignore that context when we confess, and that means that we cannot simply ignore the language in which our tradition and the larger community has confessed its faith. Just to make things really complicated, however, part of our tradition is that we have always been finding new ways to confess our faith—"always reformed, always reforming." So we need to find ways that (1) confess our own faith, honestly, while (2) remembering the ways in which we belong to a tradition and a larger community, including the fact that (3) change is itself part of the tradition in which we stand. We seek to confess not merely *a* Reformed faith but *the* Reformed faith, but we will always confess only *a* version of *the* faith. When *a* version becomes so idiosyncratic that it is no longer *the* faith is a question with which we must constantly struggle. The best advice comes from the authors of the Barmen Declaration, in words written in the face of the threat of Nazi persecution:

> If you find that we are speaking contrary to Scripture, then do not listen to us! But if you find that we are taking our stand upon Scripture, then let no fear or temptation keep you from treading with us the path of faith and obedience to the Word of God, in order that God's people be of one mind upon earth. (8.04)

And we are most faithful to scripture when we are faithful to Jesus Christ, to whom scripture witnesses, "the one Word of God which we have to hear and which we have to trust and obey in life and in death" (8.11). No human words, certainly not those of confessions, much less those of commentaries on confessions, can be our final guide. If we find that faithfulness to Jesus Christ requires a radical break with some aspects of our tradition, then we will have to make the radical break.

Those of us who are ordained promise at our ordinations to be "guided" by the *Book of Confessions,* and the image of a guide is a good one. No human guides are infallible, but good ones are wise and have often been over the ground before. We would be foolish not to listen to what they say. And we would also be foolish to make *them* the Lord we worship and serve.

Notes

Preface

1. Lukas Vischer, ed., *Reformed Witness Today* (Bern: Evangelische Arbeitsstelle Oekumene Schweiz, 1982).

Chapter 1

1. John H. Leith, ed., *Creeds of the Churches* (Atlanta: John Knox Press, 3d ed., 1982), pp. 116–17.

2. Guideline 2.c, *Minutes of the 197th General Assembly of the Presbyterian Church (U.S.A.)*, 1985, Part I: *Journal*, para. 32.012, p. 420.

3. John Calvin, *Institutes* 1.13.19. The passage he cites from Gregory of Nazianzus is in "On Holy Baptism," oration 40.41. See *Nicene and Post-Nicene Fathers*, 2d ser., vol. 7 (Grand Rapids: Wm. B. Eerdmans Publishing Co., 1957), p. 375.

Chapter 2

1. From the Council of Chalcedon, 451.

Chapter 3

1. See, for instance, Irenaeus, *Against Heresies* 5.19, in *Early Christian Fathers*, ed. Cyril C. Richardson (New York: Macmillan Co., 1970), pp. 389–91.

Chapter 4

1. One of Cicero's orations conveys the Roman horror of

crucifixion: "Let even the name of the cross be kept away not only from the bodies of the citizens of Rome, but also from their thought, sight, and hearing" (*Pro Rabirico* 5.16).

2. Raymond E. Brown, *The Gospel According to John,* vol. 1 (Garden City, N.Y.: Doubleday & Co., 1966), p. lxxi.

3. Jürgen Moltmann, *The Crucified God,* trans. R. A. Wilson and John Bowden (New York: Harper & Row, 1974), pp. 145–46.

4. C. S. Lewis, *Mere Christianity* (London: Geoffrey Bles, 1952), p. 42.

5. John Calvin, Commentary on Galatians 2:21, trans. William Pringle, *Calvin's Commentaries* (Grand Rapids: Baker Book House, 1989), vol. 21, p. 77.

6. Calvin, Commentary on Romans 5:10, trans. John Owen, *Calvin's Commentaries,* vol. 19, p. 198.

Chapter 5

1. Latin text, trans. Francis Pott (1861); *The Presbyterian Hymnal* (Louisville, Ky.: Westminster/John Knox Press, 1990), #119.

2. Presbyterian Church in the Republic of Korea, "New Confession" (1972) 4.5, in Vischer, ed., *Reformed Witness Today,* p. 79.

3. Presbyterian Church in the United States, "A Declaration of Faith" (1976) 4.5, in Vischer, ed., *Reformed Witness Today,* pp. 243–44.

Chapter 6

1. See Sallie McFague, *Metaphorical Theology* (Philadelphia: Fortress Press, 1982), pp. 145–92; Paul Tillich, *Systematic Theology* (Chicago: University of Chicago Press, 1951), vol. 1, pp. 240–41.

2. Alice Walker, *The Color Purple* (New York: Pocket Books, 1982), p. 202.

3. See also the Heidelburg Catechism:

"Q. 26. What do you believe when you say:'I believe in God the Father Almighty, Maker of heaven and earth'?

"A. That the eternal Father of Our Lord Jesus Christ . . . is

for the sake of Christ his Son my God and my Father. . . .
Moreover, whatever evil he sends upon me in this troubled life
he will turn to my good, for he is able to do it, being almighty
God, and is determined to do it, being a faithful Father"
(4.026).

Here "Father" and "God" seem to be alternative names.

4. Karl Barth, *Church Dogmatics,* vol. 1, part 1, trans. G. T.
Thomson (Edinburgh: T. & T. Clark, 1936), p. 447.

5. "For all who are led by the Spirit of God are children of
God. For you did not receive a spirit of slavery to fall back into
fear, but you have received a spirit of adoption. When we cry,
'Abba! Father!' it is that very Spirit bearing witness with our
spirit that we are children of God, and if children, then heirs,
heirs of God and joint heirs with Christ" (Rom. 8:14–17).

6. See Joachim Jeremias, *New Testament Theology,* trans.
John Bowden (New York: Charles Scribner's Sons, 1971), pp.
61–67; Edward Schillebeeckx, *Jesus,* trans. Hubert Hoskins
(New York: Seabury Press, 1979), pp. 256–69; Günther
Bornkamm, *Jesus of Nazareth,* trans. Irene and Fraser McLuskey
(New York: Harper & Row, 1960), pp. 124–29.

Chapter 7

1. C. S. Lewis, *The Four Loves* (San Diego: Harcourt Brace
Jovanovich, 1971), p. 176.

2. Athanasius, "On the Incarnation of the Word" 1.4, trans.
Archibald Robertson, *Nicene and Post-Nicene Fathers,* 2d ser.,
vol. 4 (Grand Rapids: Wm. B. Eerdmans Publishing Co.,
1957), p. 36.

3. Jürgen Moltmann, *God in Creation,* trans. Margaret Kohl
(San Francisco: Harper & Row, 1985), p. 3.

4. Plotinus, *The Enneads* 6.9.11, trans. Stephen MacKenna
(Boston: Charles T. Branford, n.d.), vol. 2, p. 253; Porphyry,
The Life of Plotinus 1, in ibid., vol. 1, p. 9.

5. Calvin, Commentary on Psalm 104:15, trans. James
Anderson, *Calvin's Commentaries,* vol. 6, p. 157.

6. Augustine, *Confessions* 10.6, trans. Rex Warner (New
York: New American Library/Mentor-Omega, 1963), p. 215.

7. Some Christians have believed that God made all the
souls at once at the beginning of time and only puts them into

bodies one at a time, at the beginning of a person's life. But the far more common Christian view, consistently held in the Reformed tradition, is that new souls come into being at the beginning of each new life. Therefore, here, the present tense "makes" is appropriate—God keeps creating new souls.

8. For what follows, see Moltmann, *God in Creation,* pp. 219–20.

9. Blaise Pascal, *Pensées,* trans. W. F. Trotter (New York: E. P. Dutton & Co., 1958), p. 97, #347.

10. Gregory of Nyssa, "On the Soul and the Resurrection," trans. William Moore, *Nicene and Post-Nicene Fathers,* 2d ser., vol. 5 (Grand Rapids: Wm. B. Eerdmans Publishing Co., 1987), p. 450.

11. H. Shelton Smith, *In His Image, But . . . : Racism in Southern Religion* (Durham, N.C.: Duke University Press, 1972).

12. "The Manual of Epictetus," trans. P. E. Matheson, in Jason L. Saunders, ed., *Greek and Roman Philosophy After Aristotle* (New York: Free Press, 1966), p. 136.

13. Calvin, Commentary on 1 John 3:17, trans. John Owen, *Calvin's Commentaries,* vol. 22, p. 220.

14. Calvin, Commentary on Ezekiel 18:7, trans. Thomas Myers, *Calvin's Commentaries,* vol. 12, p. 224.

15. "A Declaration of Faith for the Church in South Africa" (1979), in Vischer, ed., *Reformed Witness Today,* p. 27.

Chapter 8

1. Calvin, *Institutes* 2.1.5., but see also Calvin, Commentary on John 3:6, trans. William Pringle (*Calvin's Commentaries,* vol. 17, p. 113), where he seems to take the opposite view.

2. Quoted in Shirley C. Guthrie, *Christian Doctrine* (Atlanta: John Knox Press, 1968), p. 213.

3. Augustine, *The City of God* 14.13, trans. Henry Bettenson (Harmondsworth, England: Penguin Books, 1976), p. 573.

4. PCUS, "A Declaration of Faith," (1976) 2.6, in Vischer, ed., *Reformed Witness Today,* p. 237.

5. For a good discussion of such issues by a member of the Committee of Fifteen, which revised this Statement, see Susan

Dunfee, *Beyond Servanthood: Christianity and the Liberation of Women* (Washington, D.C.: University Press of America, 1989).

6. Reinhold Niebuhr, *The Nature and Destiny of Man,* vol. 1 (New York: Charles Scribner's Sons, 1964), p. 194.

7. Calvin, Commentary on Genesis 9:6, trans. John King, *Calvin's Commentaries,* vol. 1, pp. 295–96.

8. Niebuhr, *The Nature and Destiny of Man,* vol. 1, p. 203.

9. *Treatises Against the Anabaptists and Against the Libertines,* ed. and trans. Benjamin Wirt Farley (Grand Rapids: Baker Book House, 1982), pp. 284–85.

10. Presbyterian Church in the Republic of Korea, "New Confession" 2.3, in Vischer, ed., *Reformed Witness Today,* p. 74.

Chapter 9

1. Calvin, Commentary on Galatians 3:23, trans. William Pringle, *Calvin's Commentaries,* vol. 21, p. 107.

2. Megillah 10b; in C. G. Montefiore and H. Loewe, *A Rabbinic Anthology* (New York: Schocken Books, 1974), p. 52.

3. See Joanna Bos, "When We Pray Our Father," *Presbyterian Survey,* May 1981, pp. 10–12.

Chapter 10

1. Karl Barth, *Learning Jesus Christ Through the Heidelberg Catechism,* trans. Shirley C. Guthrie, Jr. (Grand Rapids: Wm. B. Eerdmans Publishing Co., 1964), p. 84.

2. Jonathan Edwards, *Representative Selections,* ed. C. Faust and T. Johnson (New York: Hill & Wang, 1935), p. 222.

3. Ibid., p. 223.

4. Max Thurian, *Our Faith,* trans. Emily Chisholm (New York: Crossroad, 1982).

5. Harold A. Carter, *The Prayer Tradition of Black People* (Valley Forge, Pa.: Judson Press, 1976), p. 57.

6. See Calvin, *Institutes* 3.1.1; and 3.2.23–24, on Christ's union with believers.

7. Barth, *Church Dogmatics,* vol. 4, part 3, trans. G. W. Bromiley (Edinburgh: T. & T. Clark, 1962), pp. 941ff. See Jan Lochman's treatment of this in the section on "Identity and

Fulfillment of the Free Human Being," in *The Faith We Confess: An Ecumenical Dogmatics,* trans. David Lewis (Philadelphia: Fortress Press, 1984), pp. 186ff.

8. Esther de Waal, *Seeking God: The Way of St. Benedict* (London: Collins/Faith Press, 1984), pp. 118–19.

Chapter 11

1. Augustine, *Commentary on John* 80.3, trans. John Gibb and James Innes, *Nicene and Post-Nicene Fathers,* 1st ser., vol. 7 (New York: Christian Literature Company, 1888), p. 344.

2. Paul Tillich, *Dynamics of Faith* (New York: Harper & Brothers, 1958) p. 42.

3. See, for instance, Heidelberg Catechism 4.074.

4. See, for instance, 1 Corinthians 14:34–35.

Chapter 12

1. See Carl Braaten, *The Apostolic Imperative* (Minneapolis: Augsburg Publishing House, 1985), especially ch. 4; and Arnold B. Lovell, ed., *Evangelism in the Reformed Tradition* (Decatur, Ga.: CTS Press, 1990).

2. Flannery O'Connor, *The Complete Short Stories* (New York: Farrar, Straus & Giroux, 1972), p. 508.

3. This, not incidentally, is the strength of H. Richard Niebuhr's argument, in *The Responsible Self,* that interpretation is fundamental to the other parts of ethical activity, namely, asking the questions of what is legal and what is feasible.

4. Paul makes the same point at considerable length in chapter 1 of 1 Corinthians. It is also the point that Calvin is making when he designates "poverty" as opposed to "pomp" as a characteristic of the true church. (See *Institutes,* Prefatory Letter to King Francis.)

5. Paul Lehmann, *Ethics in a Christian Context* (New York: Harper & Row, 1963).

Chapter 13

1. Martin Luther King, Jr., *Strength to Love* (Philadelphia: Fortress Press, 1981), pp. 63–65. The dedication of this volume is "To my Mother and my Father whose deep commitment to

the Christian faith and unswerving devotion to its timeless principles have given me an inspiring example of the Strength to Love."

2. There is a kind of carryover here—into the view of the sacredness of the common life—of the monastic vow of "stability": to be active in love where you are and to accept with gratitude the locus of your life as the field of your vocation.

3. *The Book of Common Worship* (Philadelphia: Board of Christian Education, Presbyterian Church in the United States of America, 1946), pp. 341–42.

4. John Ciardi, *39 Poems* (New Brunswick, N.J.: Rutgers University Press, 1959), p. 13.

Chapter 14

1. Barth, *Church Dogmatics,* vol. 3, part 3, trans. G. W. Bromiley and R. J. Ehrlich (Edinburgh: T. & T. Clark, 1961), p. 90.

For Further Reading

Guides to the *Book of Confessions*

Dowey, Edward A., Jr. *A Commentary on the Confession of 1967 and an Introduction to the "Book of Confessions"* (Philadelphia: Westminster Press, 1968. OP.). A detailed commentary on the Confession of 1967 and an introduction to earlier confessions, written by the moderator of the committee that drafted C-67.

Eberts, Harry W., Jr. *We Believe: A Study of the Book of Confessions for Church Officers* (Philadelphia: Geneva Press, 1987).

Keesecker, William F. *A Layperson's Guide to the Theology of the Book of Confessions of the United Presbyterian Church in the United States of America* (New York: Office of the General Assembly, 1976. OP.). The author, a lifelong pastor, was a member of the Committee of Fifteen.

Rogers, Jack. *Presbyterian Creeds: A Guide to the Book of Confessions* (Philadelphia: Westminster Press, 1985). Written by a member of the committee that drafted the Brief Statement. A supplement, which will be a concluding chapter about the Brief Statement to be included in subsequent editions, is currently available from the publisher.

Collections of Confessions

Gerrish, B. A. *The Faith of Christendom* (Cleveland: Meridian Books, 1963).

Leith, John H., ed. *Creeds of the Churches: A Reader in Christian Doctrine from the Bible to the Present* (Atlanta: John Knox Press, 3d ed., 1982). Leith and Gerrish both served on the committee that drafted the Brief Statement. These two volumes provide parallel collections of confessional documents from the whole Christian tradition.

Vischer, Lukas, ed. *Reformed Witness Today* (Bern: Evangelische Arbeitsstelle Oekumene Schweiz, 1982). Confessional statements from all around the world written by Reformed churches or at unions of churches in the last forty years. One can usually obtain copies from the Office of the General Assembly.

Background for A Brief Statement of Faith

Stotts, Jack L., and Jane Dempsey Douglass, eds. *To Confess the Faith Today* (Louisville, Ky.: Westminster/John Knox Press, 1990). Articles by seven members of the drafting committee on the context and content of the Brief Statement.

Index of Names
and Subjects

Index of Scripture References